Also by Deirdre Imus

The Imus Ranch: Cooking for Kids and Cowboys

green this!

volume one

greening your cleaning

deirdre imus

simon & schuster

new york   london   toronto   sydney

Simon & Schuster Paperbacks
1230 Avenue of the Americas
New York, NY 10020

The letters and conversations that appear in the book are based on real communications received by the author. However, in some cases they have been edited, reconstructed, and/or combined from several communications.

First Simon & Schuster trade paperback edition April 2007

SIMON & SCHUSTER Paperbacks and colophon are registered trademarks of Simon & Schuster, Inc.

Designed by Karolina Harris

For information about special discounts for bulk purchases, please contact Simon & Schuster Special Sales at 1-800-456-6798 or business@simonandschuster.com

This book was printed using post-consumer recycled chlorine-free paper and environmentally friendly inks.

Manufactured in the United States of America

10   9   8   7   6   5   4   3   2   1

Library of Congress Cataloging-in-Publication Data Control Number: 2007007882

ISBN-13: 978-1-4165-4055-7
ISBN-10:   1-4165-4055-5

acknowledgments

Thanks to Laura Moser, my writer, and Amanda Murray, our editor. Both were wonderful to work with.

I adore and thank my agent, Esther Newberg. Also thanks to Andy Barzvi at ICM for finding Laura Moser.

Thanks to everyone at the Deirdre Imus Environmental Center for Pediatric Oncology at Hackensack University Medical Center: Mark Blaire, Bonnie Eskenazi, Jim Ronchi, Erin Ihde, LaRae Muse, and David Marks for all their help with research; Mark Blaire for help with all the details; and Bonnie Eskenazi for her continued dedication to all the work we do at the center.

I owe a special thanks to John Ferguson, President and CEO of Hackensack University Medical Center, for believing in my vision of seeing hospitals as clean and green places of healing. Our Greening the Cleaning program has been made possible because of his courageous leadership.

My friend David Jurist has provided practical, emotional, and financial support for all our efforts at Hackensack from day one.

Don and Wyatt are my life. I thank them for all their love and support and I will continue to provide for them as green an environment as possible, whether they like it or not.

contents

two: one change at a time

The frog does not drink up the pond in which he lives.

SIOUX

one:
why green?

Chapter 1

A New Meaning of Clean

Our Most Precious Natural Resource

We all want the best for our children—the best schools, the best doctors, the best foods. But often, we give little thought to the environment where our children live, and the quality of the air they breathe. Some of us smoke with our children sitting right next to us. We bring home dinner from a fast food restaurant because it's cheap, or zap leftover lasagna in the microwave because it's convenient. We spray pesticides on the lawns where our children play, and set off roach bombs in the rooms where they sleep. We use chlorine bleach, and ammonia, and dozens of other toxic chemicals to clean the clothes our children wear, and the plates they eat off, and the carpets they lounge on to watch TV.

We make these compromises every day, not because we don't care about our children—on the contrary. More than anything, we want our homes to be clean and sanitary, safe havens where our children can thrive. We compromise because we're busy and exhausted and overcommitted. Taking constant shortcuts seems the only way to manage our hectic lives.

But the time has come to slow down and start paying more attention—our children's futures depend on it. We live in a world polluted by toxins. We're exposed to pesticides and carcinogens in the foods we eat and the clothes we wear; in the air we breathe, the water we drink, and the substances we use to clean our houses. The deadly chemical cocktail building up in our bodies is causing us great harm, manifesting itself in everything from asthma to cancer. Toxins are ravaging our lives—and even more so the lives of our children. Because they are smaller and still developing, they are far more vulnerable than we are to toxic exposures, yet they are assaulted at identical levels.

Now, as a result, their health is suffering. In the United States, childhood cancers, now the leading cause of death by disease for children between the ages of one and nineteen, increased by approximately 21 percent between 1975 and 1998. Certain other cancers—brain tumors, leukemia, acute lymphoblastic leukemia (ALL), and central nervous system malignancies—are growing even faster, at rates of about 30 percent over the last two decades. The National Cancer Institute estimates that these rates will continue to grow an additional one percent every year. And that's just the beginning. Over the past decade, we've seen a sixfold increase in attention deficit hyperactivity disorder (ADHD). An appalling American diet has produced an obesity epidemic, and diabetes is at nearly epidemic proportions as well. Childhood asthma is the leading cause of emergency room visits and absenteeism in schools. Rates of autism are rising fast, and rheumatoid arthritis has become the third-most-common chronic childhood disorder. Premature births, problems conceiving, and birth defects are all on the rise.

It's no secret that environmental factors contribute to many of these extremely serious health issues. But even as our bodies rebel against toxins, we continue exposing ourselves to them recklessly, without pausing to consider how our snap decisions might affect our health, or the health of future generations. Most of us feel helpless when confronted with these terrifying realities. We shrug off the health crisis our kids are facing as beyond our individual control.

I'm here to tell you that we can take action to improve this situation, and it's much easier than you might think. As consumers, we have the power to control the level of toxins that enter our homes. With a little knowledge, we can give our families a much healthier life.

Rethinking how we clean our homes is, to me, the most logical place to begin this process. After all, unlike so many other modern conveniences, we don't use chemical cleaning products to save time or money. We use them because our mothers used them—because, quite simply, we don't know any better.

Throughout the book, I've tried to identify ingredients that may be harmful to you and your family. Some of my assertions might be controversial; the manufacturers of these products will insist that they have been tested and are safe when used as directed. But I don't think that should be the end of the inquiry. Even if the products I discuss are not necessarily toxic to all people in all circumstances, they do all contain potentially dangerous substances. Obviously, the hazards depend on many factors, including how concentrated the chemicals are, and how long we're exposed to them, but can we really afford to take risks with our children's health? Even if the phenol in a single squirt of air freshener isn't immediately harmful, the amount in a bottle is likely to be toxic if your child ingests it. And kids love to sample everything they can get their hands on.

I am also concerned that there has not been sufficient testing to determine the harm to the environment or the long-term ill-health effects of exposure to commercial cleaning products. What little we do know is frightening, so instead of gambling with our children's future, I really recommend using nontoxic alternatives whenever they're available.

Did you know that the ingredients in many common household cleaners—laundry and dishwashing detergents, glass and tile cleaners, air fresheners, furniture polish, carpet shampoo—have been linked to a number of serious childhood health disorders, everything from asthma to cancer? If not, it's not your fault: The manufacturers of these familiar items never tell us that their products are packed with potential carcinogens, neurotoxins, mutagens, teratogens, and endocrine and hormone disrupters. Misleading or incomplete labels can fool even the most conscientious moms.

These companies have no incentive to enlighten us. Think about it. If more of us knew that the cleaning products we depend on every day contained potentially dangerous chemicals, we'd surely stop buying them immediately. And if we did that, these hugely powerful corporations would be forced to change their business practices, or start losing money fast. But what's more important in the end—these companies' profits, or our children's futures?

As a culture, I think we're all looking for ways to live healthier and get closer to nature, whether consciously or not. We desperately want to lower our toxic burden, not add to it every time we do the dishes or disinfect the toilet. Unfortunately, that's exactly what we're doing every time we clean our homes with chemicals.

The good news is that there is a safer way to keep your homes germ and dirt free—without sacrificing quality, or investing any extra time or money. There's no reason to lower your standards or empty your wallet to protect your children's health. No reason, either, to feel stressed by the changes I'm proposing you make. I know from experience that stress paralyzes people, and I can't emphasize enough that real change occurs slowly, one tweak at a time.

I repeat: This doesn't have to be a big project. I'm not asking you to put your life on hold, or do weeks of research, or overhaul your entire household. I've written this book to demystify the process for you, to give you realistic steps that will empower you to make the first small changes.

The more you learn, the more you'll understand how much common sense my whole approach makes. You'll begin to ask: If nontoxic products exist that work as effectively as—and sometimes even more effectively than—the synthetic cleaners I grew up with, why would I knowingly expose my children to harmful toxins? Why not eliminate all traces of chemicals that might make my kids sick or harm the environment?

As parents, we have a responsibility to start asking these questions—and to start demanding answers. We need to equip ourselves with this information so that we can make the right choices for our kids. Children are our most precious natural resource. They don't have a voice of their own. It's time we spoke up on their behalf. For their sake, I encourage you to make the commitment to a healthier life today.

Going Off Autopilot

Cleaning is a necessity, a basic fact of life. Whether you're a single mom, or a student, or a bachelor, whether you do your own cleaning or pay someone else to do it for you, sooner or later you have no choice in the matter.

How you clean, on the other hand, is entirely up to you. With a few simple actions, you can decide if, when cleaning your house, you are going to nurture or pollute your family. You can choose whether the cleaning products you bring home will be a primary source of good or of bad, of safety or contamination.

But what does "clean" really mean? What does clean even smell like?

Sadly, most of us have never given these basic questions much thought. If you're like me, you probably grew up associating "clean" with the chemical stench of your mother's tried-and-true cleaning products. If our bathroom reeked of ammonia or pine or chlorine bleach, then I assumed that it was clean, germ free, sanitized. To me, clean equaled chemical.

This is a common, but dangerous, mistake. When I got to college, I

had already made a commitment to healthy living. As a competitive run-
ner, I paid close attention to the foods that I put into my body. But it
hadn't yet occurred to me that there might also be a connection between
my performance on the track and the products I used to clean my living
space.

So when I walked down that mysterious aisle of the grocery store
for the first time, I went right on autopilot, reaching for the same brands
that I remembered my mother and grandmother buying year after year.
Like most people, I confused familiarity with safety.

Back then, I had no idea that I was breathing in potentially toxic
fumes whenever I mopped, or scrubbed my toilet, or cleaned my oven. I
didn't realize that most commercial dishwasher powders contain some
bleach, which combines with hot water to emit chlorine vapors that can
be absorbed right into our skin and lungs. Or that some upholstery shampoos can damage the nerves, liver, and kidneys. I definitely didn't know
that the ingredients in many air fresheners might cause cancer.

Most of you don't consider these hazards every time you dart into
the store to grab a new box of laundry detergent. You're probably like I
was: Because you have a million other things on your mind, you default
to buying the exact same products—or maybe the new-and-improved
version of those exact same products—that your mothers relied on when
you were growing up. What worked for them will work for you—right?

But there's a major problem with this whole scenario. Over the
last two decades, we've learned a lot of disturbing information about
the chemicals in these cleaning products. We know that, despite the
proven hazards of their main ingredients, very few conventional household cleaners have ever been evaluated for their long-term impact on
human—and particularly children's—health. Untested combinations of
chemicals hit the shelves of supermarkets and drugstores with no inter-
ference from the government.

Why, when they're hurting us like this, do we insist on sticking to the same old toxic cleaning products? It defies common sense. These substances are making us sick. They're making our kids sick, our pets sick, and our environment sick.

Given the state of our children's health, we can no longer afford to ignore these dangers. Each and every one of us needs to start asking, as I did almost twenty years ago: Does the fact that my mom used this product prove that it's good for me? What do I know about this product's ingredients, and the impact those ingredients will have on my family? And why is it so hard to get answers? Why would I buy a product when I turn it over to read the list of ingredients and can't even find out what's in it?

As I said earlier, that's all I want you to do at this stage—just start asking the questions. For me, this is the single most important step of the whole greening process: becoming aware of the problem. Once you understand how these environmental toxins affect you, the rest will fall into place.

Over time, you'll come to realize that the way your mother cleaned might not have been the best or the safest or even the most sanitary way to clean. In fact, the old way of cleaning might actually be dirty.

Now, I love my mother dearly, and to her credit, over the years she has been 100 percent right about almost everything. She's also incredibly open to new ideas, which is one reason I admire her so much. As soon as I educated her about the dangers of toxic cleaning products, she wasted no time in going green. I'll bet your moms will do the same, and not because they're tree huggers or radical environmentalists. They'll make the switch because nontoxic products work better, and they make you feel better, too: no more unpleasant odors and allergies, no more watery eyes and rashes every time you reach for the scouring sponge. We've come to assume that cleaning our houses should make us cough and sneeze and tear—that it's somehow a form of physical punishment.

A woman in Milwaukee, Wisconsin, recently wrote me about the unpleasant side effects she experienced whenever she cleaned her house: "I'd always assumed that housecleaning was supposed to make my eyes water and my skin break out into a nasty rash. I was used to coughing and sneezing whenever I cleaned—I thought it was all part of the process. But now that I'm using nontoxic products, I'm happy to report that I can breathe easily as I clean—and my hands no longer get red and irritated. My whole relationship with housecleaning has changed completely."

It can all change for you, too—but only if you switch off the autopilot. Quit sleepwalking through your daily chores. Green cleaning isn't just healthy—it can also be pretty fun. Who knows? Once you get rid of all that nasty-smelling toxic stuff, you might start to enjoy yourself.

Less Is More

Once you learn the facts about chemical cleaning products, you have a responsibility to change how you clean. At the same time, it's important that you implement these changes at your own pace, one at a time. Real, long-term changes aren't the product of dramatic resolutions, but of gradual, barely perceptible adjustments in attitude and lifestyle made over the years.

Think about all the fad diets out there. Do any of them actually work? Yes, if you eat only cabbage soup for a month, you'll probably lose weight. But what happens when the month is over? Chances are you'll go back to the same old eating habits that inspired you to go on a diet in the first place. Wouldn't it make more sense to educate yourself about good nutrition and exercise, and try to live healthier?

In this and everything else, the most extreme measures tend to be the shortest-lived, while the most enduring changes are the ones we hardly even notice at first.

So take it slow. Our lives are complicated enough as it is; no need to go overboard. I know from my own experience—and from talking to my mom and sister and close friends—that most mothers are too busy to sit down for five minutes at a stretch, much less completely revamp their households overnight.

Trust me, that's not what I'm asking you to do. You don't have to toss out every product under your kitchen sink and start over from zero—that would be completely impractical and beside the point. I don't expect you to give up paper towels or make all your own cleaning products from scratch—who has time for that? I'm not demanding that you become a children's health expert or read a bunch of books about healthy living. I'm just suggesting that you pay a little more attention to the world around you. Question your old assumptions. Look closer at labels—what they do and don't say. Learn not to be deceived by flashy marketing and packaging. Educate yourself about all the healthy options out there already.

As you read through this book, you'll pick up many simple practices that will make your home a healthier, more truly clean place. But remember—please don't attempt to adopt them all in one swoop. If you do, you'll get overwhelmed, and as soon as that happens, it's all over.

Once you green one aspect of your life, I can guarantee that you'll want to continue. Going green is a constantly evolving process that all follows from that first tiny step. Just as small, everyday exposures to toxic chemicals can severely damage your health over the long term, small, everyday improvements can yield powerful long-term benefits. If you make just one simple change—for example, trading your usual glass cleaner for a nontoxic one—you'll notice a difference in your environment right away.

From there, you might feel ready to move on to the next small change. Maybe the next time you run out of your favorite automatic dishwasher detergent, you'll decide to replace it with a nontoxic, phosphate- and bleach-free product. Maybe you'll feel good knowing that the consequences of this choice will extend way beyond your immediate physical environment. You won't just be exposing your kids to fewer toxins. You'll also be saving gallons and gallons of water every day from contamination.

You may also come to appreciate how green cleaning simplifies your life. We've gotten into the habit of buying two, three, or even four separate products to perform the same job. Why? Because we're not exactly sure what's in these products, or what they're supposed to do. Our cleaning has gotten out of control, it's not good for us—overcleaning is one of the main reasons we have so many allergies. This overkill is hurting our children and our planet, and adding more complications to our already crazy lives. We need to stop loading up on identical products that serve no beneficial purpose.

Eventually, you may discover that going green involves more than making concrete changes. Pretty soon, your whole mind-set will be transformed for the better. Everything fits together into a web here: Before you know it, you'll have significantly improved your health and overall quality of life. But I can't emphasize enough that green cleaning is just a tool. If you follow my simple suggestions, you'll already be leading a healthier life and providing your kids with a better future. I promise you—it's the easiest thing in the world. And it all starts with redefining what clean really means.

Chapter 2

My Commitment

The Web of Life

People often ask me how I describe myself. I've been given various labels over the years: environmentalist, children's advocate, green activist, green advocate, humanitarian, children's health expert, philanthropist. While in some sense I play all these roles, I don't personally subscribe to any of those labels. I didn't go to college to prepare for this work. I'm not a chemist or a doctor. But I have devoted myself to these issues full-time, because I thought it made common sense to do so. My own path to green living reflects this logic. I cleaned up my life because cleaning up my life made sense.

As an athlete, I educated myself about food. To improve my performance on the track, I made a commitment to eating better. I eliminated fast foods, like hamburgers and French fries, from my diet. I also started asking questions: Where does the food we eat come from? How is it grown? Is it good for me? What impact does my diet have on the world around me? The more I educated myself about the chemicals used in agriculture, the more I wanted to know about the big picture. I started reading up on how products are made—not just foods, but our shampoos, and baby-care products, and building materials, and clothing—and how these products affect both human health and the environment.

And little by little, even after I quit running track competitively, I kept making adjustments to reduce my toxic burden. By 1990, I was a vegetarian and eating only organic foods to limit my exposure to pesticides. Around the same time, I quit using chemical products to clean my home. There weren't many green cleaning products on the market in those days, so I experimented with household staples like baking soda, vinegar, and lemon juice. I also paid more attention to the way my clothes and sheets were made, and tried to buy organic fabrics whenever possible.

Later, when I became pregnant with my son, Wyatt, I became even more dedicated to these choices. I wanted my child to grow up happy and strong, and I've always believed in leading by example. Living green seemed the best way to give my son a healthy future. For my son's sake, I vowed to take personal responsibility for my everyday actions and lifestyle. I realized that, whether we like it our not, the way we live has a huge impact on our kids as well as on our water systems, our soil, plants, and wildlife—the whole environment.

As it is, our out-of-control dependency on electricity, gas, and toxins, toxins, toxins is destroying not just our health, but the entire planet. Nothing is safe from contamination. Mercury, a toxic by-product of the coal-burning process, is building up in the fatty tissue of fish all over the world. Scientists have found industrial chemicals in the ice in Antarctica, and polar bears with dangerously high levels of dioxin and polychlorinated biphenyls (PCBs) in their blood. Natural forces—wind and water and air—are transporting these toxins hundreds and thousands of miles from us, to the very ends of the earth.

I frequently think about the Lakota Indian saying "Mitake oyasin" (*mee-tahk-wee ah-say*), which roughly translates to: "We're all one with creation." Now more than ever before, we're all the same, all connected in this great web of life. It's time we started taking better care of one another.

The Imus Ranch

In 1992, I began helping my husband with his annual "radiothon" for kids with cancer. Even after years of reading up on environmental issues, I was shocked to learn how huge a role toxic exposures play in incidences of pediatric cancer. Collectively, fewer than 10 percent of all malignancies are thought to involve inherited mutations. Today, most scientists believe that environmental factors cause or contribute to the remaining 80 or 90 percent of childhood cancers.

For over five years, my husband and I discussed different ways we could help these kids. Then one morning, when I was pregnant with Wyatt, my husband had the brilliant idea that over time evolved into the Imus Ranch.

The Imus Ranch began as the ultimate leap of faith. With the generous support of people all over the country, we built the 4,000-acre ranch in Ribera, New Mexico, about an hour's drive from Santa Fe. By 1998, children suffering from cancer and various life-threatening blood disorders, such as sickle-cell anemia, and children who have lost a brother or sister to SIDS (sudden infant death syndrome), were traveling from all over to experience life on our authentic 1880s-style working cattle ranch.

From the beginning, we wanted the Imus Ranch to be different from any place these kids had ever known. My husband and I had noticed that all too often, kids with cancer get treated differently from other kids. Everyone in their lives—their parents, teachers, doctors, even peers—coddle them, sometimes with good reason.

At the ranch, we took the opposite tack: Instead of placing limitations on these kids, we put them to work. Through a demanding program that promotes perseverance, discipline, and a strong work ethic, these kids get their sense of purpose back. They regain their self-esteem, dignity, and confidence. They discover that they can do anything any other kid can do, sometimes more. In pushing them to work hard, and treating them not as china dolls but as regular kids, we remind them that they're defined by more than their disease.

To support their health, we've created a pristine environment, eliminating as many indoor and outdoor toxins as possible. We've built every structure "green," with completely nontoxic materials and paints. The food we serve—most of which we grow in greenhouses on the ranch—is organic and vegan. We use only Imus GTC (greening the cleaning) products made from readily biodegradable, naturally derived materials free of all known or suspected carcinogenic substances. We never allow pesticides or synthetic chemicals of any kind in our gardening, farming, infrastructure, or plant maintenance.

As always, common sense motivated every single one of these decisions. If you have any choice in the matter, why would you expose children—especially children with cancer, whose immune systems are already compromised—to contaminants that might further damage their health? Why would you spray soccer fields and lawns with pesticides that impair brain functioning and have proven links to serious learning disabilities? Why feed kids junk food—processed white bread, potato chips, candy—that provides no nourishment? Just because it's easier, cheaper? Grown-ups would never accept that kind of treatment—why should our kids settle for it? Especially these kids. They've already overcome so many obstacles at such an early age—more than most people endure in a lifetime. Shouldn't we be making every effort to protect them?

Greening Hackensack and Beyond

My summers at the ranch got me thinking. Most of the kids who came out to New Mexico had spent a good chunk of their youth in hospitals.

Because I've always believed that your physical environment can either harm you or heal you, I started wondering what these pediatric hospitals were like on the inside. They were like second homes to many of these kids. But were they nurturing? Were these hospitals doing everything within their powers to give these kids their lives back?

I soon found out that hospitals still relied exclusively on chemical cleaning agents. And because they used such huge quantities of cleaning products, hospitals are a leading source of toxic emissions in the country.

To me, this made no sense. Chemical cleaning products seemed to undermine the very purpose of a hospital. Think about it. You only go to a hospital when you're already sick. The synthetic chemicals in these products weaken the immune system and contribute to indoor air pollution, which has been linked to respiratory problems and other serious diseases. So if you're exposed to toxins within this sensitive environment, you're likely to get even sicker.

In December of 2000, I spoke with John Ferguson, president of the Hackensack University Medical Center, about the dangers of introducing disease-causing agents into a health care setting. We talked about indoor air pollution, and the threats toxic cleaning products pose to patients'—particularly children's—health. To my surprise, John was immediately open to my suggestion: that we revolutionize the Hackensack hospital—the fourth largest independent hospital in the country, with approximately nine thousand employees—by converting its massive cleaning system to an environmentally responsible Greening the Cleaning program.

It was this initiative that launched the Deirdre Imus Environmental Center for Pediatric Oncology in early 2001. With an assembled team of experts, we set up shop in Hackensack and got to work immediately. Our first step was to develop nontoxic products that met my high standards.

From the beginning, I laid out a few simple ground rules. Our green products had to be at least as effective as the leading toxic brands. Obviously, efficacy was the number one requirement here—hospitals simply can't take risks when it comes to infectious disease. For our plan to be at all viable, green cleaning had to work.

Second, our products had to be safe for both humans and the environment. They had to reduce the level of toxins in our bodies and the level of waste in our environment. We resolved to use all-natural, renewable, and biodegradable ingredients whenever we could.

Last but not least, our products had to cost roughly the same as their chemical counterparts. I know that both individuals and institutions make decisions on the basis of price, and like most hospitals, Hackensack operates on a careful budget. Green cleaning wouldn't last very long if it was too expensive to implement.

In the spring of 2001, the results of our green cleaning experiment exceeded even our most optimistic expectations. After conducting some preliminary tests, hospital administrators were thrilled to report that our green products passed with flying colors. In fact, some of our green cleaning agents worked even better than the toxic formulas the hospital had previously used. And because we reduced the total number of cleaning products from twenty-two to eleven, we were also saving Hackensack both money and storage space.

Our greening led to other, less predictable benefits, too. The morale of everyone at the hospital got a huge boost overnight. People felt more energetic going into work every morning, and the janitorial staff appreciated the measures taken to safeguard their health and well-being. These improvements rippled into the larger community as well. By eliminating the chemical cleaning products used at the Hackensack University Medical Center, we also reduced the toxins in the Hackensack water supply. Just like that, the entire town was a healthier place to live.

Having witnessed these remarkable results, the people who run the Hackensack University Medical Center now approach every decision from a holistic viewpoint. They're constantly asking, "How will this choice affect our patients? How will it affect our staff? How will it affect the Hackensack community, and finally, how will it affect the environment as a whole?" My own evolution was similar: from an interest in improving my diet, I soon came to examine the impact of all my lifestyle choices on the world around me.

Our work at Hackensack has proved that making these changes isn't difficult. If such a small adjustment can transform an enormous hospital system, just imagine what it can do to your home.

Expanding the Mission

Since we greened Hackensack in 2001, the Deirdre Imus Environmental Center for Pediatric Oncology has won numerous awards. We've gone on to green thousands of facilities, many of them hospitals, government facilities, businesses, airports, and schools. We've greened millions of square feet for several hundred clients all over the country.

In addition to greening institutions, we have also developed an incredibly successful retail line of nontoxic cleaning products: Imus GTC Citrus Sage All-Purpose Cleaner, Glass and Window Cleaner, and laundry liquid profits from our institution line go to educational programs and research to help prevent the spread of pediatric cancer and other health issues with our children. One hundred percent of the profits of these sales goes to the Imus cattle ranch for kids with cancer.

The Greening the Cleaning Program has caught on so fast for a simple reason: Greening makes sense. Institutions that use nontoxic cleaning products improve people's lives and—maybe more surprisingly—they also save money. People tend to assume that nontoxic products cost more, but my environmental center has proved over and over that the exact opposite is true. Every single one of our clients has seen big savings in cleaning costs, anywhere from 3 to 75 percent. Hackensack now spends about 15 percent less on cleaning, which is a significant savings for the largest provider of inpatient and outpatient services in the state of New Jersey. Because institutions, like people, don't always give much thought to organization or method, they end up wasting a lot of money over the years. We teach our clients how to implement an extremely time- and cost-effective cleaning system. People who use our products in their homes also save money.

While making these nontoxic products available to more and more individuals and institutions, my center took on a larger goal as well: to identify, control, and ultimately eliminate hazardous environmental factors that may cause pediatric cancer and other health problems in our children. To achieve this, we've focused on two concrete objectives: first, to educate parents, children, and the public at large about unhealthy foods and toxic chemicals in our environment, and to help them find healthy alternatives. Our second goal is to serve as a voice in shaping policy decisions that affect children's environmental health.

Respected authorities have identified the most prevalent environmental threats to children, including:

- Mercury (in all its forms)
- Toxic cleaning products
- PCBs (polychlorinated biphenyls)
- Lead
- Air pollutants such as dioxins, volatile organic compounds (VOCs), asbestos
- Environmental and/or tobacco smoke
- Pesticides sprayed in the home and on the lawn

- Pesticides used in lice shampoos
- Pesticides in food and water
- Drinking water contaminants
- Industrial emissions
- Chemicals and chemical exposures from cleaning products

Now obviously, it's not always possible to eliminate all of these toxic exposures—you can't just move from your urban apartment building to a serene rural farmhouse. But with very little effort, you can greatly limit your exposure to dangerous pesticides and chemicals. Through radio, television, the Internet, and a speakers' bureau, we're educating parents on the essential preventative measures they can take to make their homes safer and more environmentally friendly.

The Center is also making significant strides in raising the awareness of lawmakers about the potential hazards of environmental toxins. In January 2005, New York Governor George Pataki issued an executive order requiring all state agencies to begin using nontoxic cleaning products. In 2006 alone, both New Jersey Governor Richard Codey and Connecticut Governor M. Jodi Rell signed executive orders directing state agencies and authorities to begin using environmentally friendly cleaning products in all municipal facilities. This year, we hope even more states will follow their lead.

But we still have a long way to go. In September of 2005, the National Institute of Child Health and Human Development announced a far-reaching plan to assess the impact of the environment on child and adult health. The National Children's Study, a provision of the Children's Health Act of 2000, was designed to examine the effects of environmental influences on the health and development of more than 100,000 children across the United States.

By tracking these children from conception to age twenty-one, the

National Children's Study aims to isolate the root causes of many common childhood conditions and disorders, including asthma, premature birth, birth defects, heart disease, leukemia, diabetes, autism, dyslexia, mental retardation, ADHD, and obesity. The study could also improve children's health by determining risk factors and other important disease triggers.

That's the good news. The bad news is that, less than a year after the study was announced, in May of 2006, the Senate moved to cut the $70 million budgeted for the study in 2007. Childhood diseases linked to environmental pollutants cost our society an estimated $54.9 billion every year, or approximately 2.8 percent of total health care costs. Spending $70 million today to identify the environmental sources of these diseases will save billions of dollars and millions of lives in the years to come.

Unfortunately, we don't live in a world where we consider children's health a priority. This is why my center is fighting so hard to keep the National Children's Study afloat. We're also working to get legislation passed that addresses the unique problems environmental pollutants pose to children. We need stronger laws that require companies to prove the safety of their products. The Environmental Protection Agency (EPA) labels thousands of chemicals as safe that have never actually been tested on human health, and this must change. Together, we can take a stand against the chemical companies lobbying so heavily against the creation of any standardized, comprehensive list of toxic hazards.

Right now, the Center is focusing on the passage of several bills geared specifically at protecting children's environmental health.

The Kid Safe Chemicals Act proposes to amend the Toxic Substances Control Act to reduce the exposure of kids, workers, and consumers to toxic chemicals, and to require more stringent and effective testing for chemicals used in consumer products. There are 80,000 chemicals currently in use in the United States, most of which are not tested for safety. In the over thirty years since the Toxic Substances Control Act was passed, the EPA has banned or restricted the use of only five chemical substances. Senator Frank Lautenberg of New Jersey is sponsoring this bill that requires all chemicals used in the home to be evaluated for their safety to children. It also mandates that companies list any ingredients in their products that are mutagens, teratogens, endocrine or hormone disrupters, neurotoxins, or carcinogens. In September 2006, California became the first state in the country to pass the Chemical Detection Bill, which requires chemical manufacturers to reveal their test methods for detecting chemicals in the air, water, and soil—and the human body. This law is an important first step in making these toxic companies take responsibility for their products.

The Combating Autism Act would amend the Public Health Services Act by expanding services for autism and autism spectrum disorders (ASDs) through research, screening, intervention, and education. Autism is one of the fastest-growing developmental disorders in the nation. According to the U.S. Centers for Disease Control and Prevention, ASDs now affect 1 in 166 children, up from 1 in 10,000 ten years ago. Politicians are beginning to acknowledge this widespread problem among children today: On August 3, 2006, the Senate unanimously passed the bill.

The Conquer Childhood Cancer Act of 2006 amends the Public Health Service Act by advancing biomedical research and treatments into pediatric cancers; ensuring that patients and families have access to current treatments and information; establishing a population-based national childhood cancer database; and promoting public awareness of pediatric cancers.

The Mercury-Free Vaccine Act of 2005 amends the Federal Food, Drug, and Cosmetic Act to designate a banned mercury-containing vaccine as adulterated. Across the country, individual states are taking a stand against manufacturing vaccines with the preservative thimerosal. Important changes are also taking place on the national level. The act also amends the Public Health Service Act to stipulate that a vaccine be banned if it contains 1 or more micrograms of mercury per dose.

These laws are just the beginning of the changes we must demand on behalf of our kids. We also need people who care enough to enforce them, and we need to practice what we preach. Our planet is a mess, and our children are sicker than they've ever been. It is not melodramatic, in my view, to suggest that this is a battle for their survival—and for ours. We need to educate the public, our school boards, our employers, and our legislators, and start working today to improve our futures.

Toxic Interruption
Chlorine/Chlorine Bleach/Chlorine By-products

The Truth About Chlorine
Chlorine and chlorinated compounds are everywhere these days. We're assaulted by chlorine around the clock: when we shower, swim, sleep, put on clothes, even cook. Since first being manufactured on an industrial scale in the early twentieth century, chlorine—which is an extremely rare gas in nature—has been used as a disinfectant in our water systems, as a bleach in the production of paper and cloth, and as the active ingredient in many different household cleaners, from laundry de-

tergents to tile scrubs. Chlorine, in fact, is one of the main smells that we've come to equate with "clean."

I cannot stress enough how dangerous this chemical can be to you and your family, especially your children. Chlorine and chlorinated compounds are toxic respiratory irritants that can severely damage the skin, eyes, and other membranes. When inhaled, chlorine fumes can irritate the nose, throat, and lungs, causing coughing, shortness of breath, phlegm buildup, and even pulmonary edema. Exposure to chlorine can also worsen already existing heart conditions or respiratory problems like asthma, chronic bronchitis, tuberculosis, and emphysema.

Chlorine, listed in the 1990 Clean Air Act as a hazardous air pollutant, is also extremely harmful to the environment and plays a big part in atmospheric ozone loss. In 1993, the American Public Health Association passed a unanimous resolution urging manufacturers to phase out the use of chlorine in consumer goods. (Not so surprisingly, big business has more or less ignored this motion.) And because chlorine ranks first in industrial injuries and deaths in the United States, the federal Occupational Safety and Health Administration monitors exposure to chlorine in the workplace.

But are those measures really enough? Now that we know how horrible chlorine is, what are we doing about it? Not very much at all. Our laws are still far too lenient when it comes to regulating this dangerous toxin. In Germany, chlorine bleach is almost impossible to find—no one uses it over there. In 1993, 40,000 household exposures to chlorine were reported to poison control centers—far more than any other chemical—and yet we're still pouring literally billions of gallons of it down our drains every day.

Why? Because chlorine is dirt-cheap. For pennies, we can clean and disinfect every surface in our house. Because chlorine costs almost nothing to manufacture, companies incorporate it into all sorts of different cleaning products: all-purpose cleaners, automatic dishwashing de-

tergents, tile scrubs, disinfectant wipes, toilet-bowl cleaners, laundry detergents, and mildew removers.

Chlorine becomes even more lethal when combined with other
chemicals including acetylene, acetate, ether, turpentine, ammonia, and
fuel gas, all of which can react explosively or form explosive compounds
with chlorine. In a washing machine, chlorine bleach can generate airborne, toxic chlorinated chemicals. When combined with acids and al-
kalis, chlorine produces a gas that can damage the deep tissues of the
lungs. Fragranced chlorine products may be even more dangerous, for
concealing the awful stench of chlorine can encourage overexposure: We
breathe it in without even realizing it.

Dangers to Children

Chlorine's bad enough for adults, but to children—who have higher
metabolic rates and a proportionally greater lung surface area—it poses
even greater threats. In 2000, U.S. poison control centers reported that
chlorine bleach was implicated in injuries to 18,863 children under the
age of six.

Because chlorine is heavier than air, it tends to collect in low-lying
areas where children, with their short stature, are more exposed to it.
The toxic vapors released when you open the dishwasher also affect children much more directly. The dishwasher opens at waist height for most
adults. But that door is right at the level of kids' mouths, which means
those chlorine vapors are going straight into their bodies. The fact that
children breathe faster in proportion to their body weight than adults
means they are more vulnerable to these types of exposure.

Chlorinated Compounds and Chlorine By-products

Over the past century, chlorine has been manipulated into many different forms, and applied to a huge variety of industrial uses. You might see

chlorine-based substances listed as hypochlorite, sodium hypochlorite, sodium dichloroisocyanurate, hydrogen chloride, hydrochloric acid. But by any other name, chlorine is just as toxic, particularly the following chlorinated by-products and compounds:

• **Trihalomethanes,** toxic by-products of chlorine disinfection of water supplies, may cause more than 10,000 cases of bladder and rectal cancer each year.

• **PCBs,** or polychlorinated biphenyls, are a chlorine-based chemical compound once used as a coolant and lubricant in electrical equipment. They have been banned since 1997 but are still present in our environment. Exposure to PCBs has been linked to lower IQs in children, deficits in intellectual ability, and poor short-term memory and attention span. PCBs also disrupt thyroid hormone homeostasis, which is a crucial part of fetal development. The Department of Health and Human Services, EPA, and International Agency for Research on Cancer have all concluded that PCBs are probably carcinogenic in humans.

• **Vinyl chloride** is a flammable gas released during the making of PVCs, a raw material used in the manufacture of everything from pacifiers and kids' toys to plastic water bottles and vinyl flooring. Vinyl chloride is a known human carcinogen that has also been linked to liver disease and other life-threatening conditions.

• **Organochlorines** are compounds that contain carbon, chlorine, and hydrogen. They don't break down easily and can be extremely dangerous to the environment. Dioxin, the most toxic man-made substance ever known, is an organochlorine.

Chlorine and Mercury

The production of chlorine bleach might also release into the environment and into your cleaning products trace amounts of mercury, a toxic, silvery metal that remains in liquid form at room temperature and evaporates quickly when exposed to the air, making it easy to inhale. Mercury is a toxic substance that can pose serious health risks to humans, adversely affecting

- The brain
- The spinal cord
- The kidneys
- The liver
- The ability to feel, see, taste, and move

If it enters a pregnant woman's body, mercury can also damage the fetus by preventing the brain and nervous system from developing normally.

Here's how the manufacture of chlorine came to produce the even more toxic mercury: Salt consists of sodium and chloride, bonded together as sodium chloride. One of the methods used to separate these elements, still used in some U.S. plants, involves sending an electrical current through them, using mercury as a conductor. This chlorine-extraction method can release mercury into the air—and into your cleaning products.

Alternatives to Chlorine

Last summer, I saw a big foldout ad in a magazine that absolutely shocked me: A series of photos showed women over the generations, all wearing white, over the line "Keeping Mothers Clean For Over 50 Years." In the last photograph, the woman was pregnant—I couldn't believe it!

I believe that at this vulnerable time, women should be minimizing if not eliminating *all* contact with potentially hazardous substances like chlorine.

Because chlorine has so many industrial uses—98 percent of the water in the United States is treated with the toxin —we probably won't be able to eliminate it from our lives completely. Still, there's absolutely no reason to introduce even more chlorine into our lives voluntarily. It's just crazy—it makes no common sense! We should be lightening our toxic burden, not adding to it. You can easily cut back on the amount of chlorine in your home:

• Disinfecting household surfaces: For your basic housecleaning, distilled white vinegar has been proven to work just as well as, and often better, than chlorine, which kills everything living, the good along with the bad. You can also use a number of essential oils—oregano, tea tree, sage, and eucalyptus, among many others—for disinfecting your home without endangering your health.

• Whitening laundry and other textiles: Chlorine bleach can damage both natural and synthetic fabrics, often destroying your clothing along with the stain. Or when used to clean a light-colored carpet, you might notice a yellowing where the stain once was. It can also cause linen, nylon, Spandex, and resin-treated permanent-press fabrics (which you should avoid anyway) to yellow irreversibly. Your clothes, linens, and carpets will last much longer if you avoid treating them with chlorine bleach products. You can buy many cost-competitive alternatives to chlorine bleach that are much gentler on your fabrics and safer on your bodies: color removers, reduction bleaches, oxygen, and other nonchlorine bleaches.

• Paper products: I've been using recycled chlorine-bleach-free writing and printer paper for years now. I also exclusively use chlorine-free paper towels, toilet paper, napkins, tampons, and pads. I never have any trouble finding these safe alternatives to chlorine-treated paper products in health-food stores. You can even get them at most of the bigger supermarkets.

"My children's school used to require that all surfaces be wiped down with chlorine bleach. Recently, out of concern for the 'potential' impact of chlorine bleach on children's health, the school changed its policy—they still spray toys with bleach, but use soap to clean tables. When I learned about this decision, I asked myself: Why, if chlorine 'might' be bad for my kids, am I still exposing them to it at home? Isn't there a safer way to prevent the spread of germs? Now, I use a nontoxic all-purpose cleaner all over my home—not just on tables and large surfaces, but on everything else my kids touch. The results are fantastic. My kids have never been healthier, and my house no longer stinks of bleach!"

Justine T., New York City

Chapter 3

The Facts

Knowing the Dangers

Once I started learning about the toxins found in common household cleaning products, I made it my mission to educate other parents as well. Knowledge is our best defense against the chemicals that are wrecking our bodies and lowering our quality of life. To protect our children, we first need to learn what we're up against.

This, I admit, is easier said than done. The EPA has estimated that there are more than 80,000 chemicals present in our environment, but that government agency has only tested a tiny fraction of them—only about 2 percent!—for their safety to humans. This oversight is scandalous, even criminal, when you consider how many diseases are caused or worsened by environmental factors. Everyday exposures to toxins can put us at risk for malignancies and other serious health problems. Environmental pollutants that contribute to these illnesses include mercury, lead, and other heavy metals; pesticides, insecticides, and fungicides; tobacco products, automotive and industrial emissions, and the chemicals found in household cleaning products. While we have some sense of the dangers these pollutants pose on an individual basis, we know next to nothing about the impact of the toxic cocktail produced by all of these chemicals together.

Since 1930, the global production of chemicals has increased over four hundred times, and the output shows no signs of tapering off anytime soon. It's shocking to me that, though we've known about the dangers of these chemicals for over thirty years now, our government is still doing so little to regulate the chemical industry. In 1976, Congress passed the Toxic Substances Control Act to allow the EPA to screen and track any industrial chemical that might pose risks to human health, but the law, weak to begin with, has never been enforced adequately.

Together, we need to work to strengthen the public health system on every level. We must conduct more research into environmental threats to children, and be more aggressive in evaluating—and limiting—the impact of these chemicals on children's health.

These toxins are everywhere, and they're hurting us. Even regular household dust can contain substances that may cause cancer and other serious diseases. And every day, our children are sprawled on the floor, breathing in those chemicals. As parents, we have a right—a responsibility—to demand that every single substance that we bring into our homes is first thoroughly tested both on adults and children. Until manufacturers conclusively prove the safety of their products, we should refuse to buy them.

The dangers associated with the chemical pollutants in household cleaning products are extremely serious. Consider this: In 1999, 92 percent of all poisonings occurred inside the home. In 2000, the Green Guide reported that cleaning products were responsible for nearly 10 percent of all toxic exposures reported to U.S. poison control centers, accounting for 206,636 calls. What's even scarier: More than half of these exposures—120,434—involved children under six.

For the sake of our children, we can't permit these numbers to continue climbing. A UCLA study indicates that "adverse health effects have been identified regarding common chemical ingredients found in

222 cleaning products." A recent survey of the 250 janitorial products used in thirty-two facilities in Richmond, California, echoes this alarming conclusion. The survey found that

- 56 percent of products require extreme care, as the ingredients can cause blindness or severe skin damage, or interfere with the endocrine system. When inhaled or absorbed through the skin, they can damage blood, liver, kidneys, nervous system, or a developing fetus.

- 7 percent of products should not be used at all, as they could cause cancer or great harm to the environment.

- The U.S. Bureau of Labor Statistics reports that 127 janitors died nationwide between 1993 and 2001 as a result of the cleaning products they were using.

Fine, you say. But I'm not a full-time janitor—I'm just a mom. I don't work with cleaning products twelve hours a day, seven days a week. These statistics have no bearing on my life.

Unfortunately, toxins won't let you off that easily. Even if you pay someone else to clean your house with chemicals, you still may be exposing yourself and your family to the risks. The chemicals in many cleaning products may leave residues all over your house that affect you whenever you eat, sleep, or even breathe. Experts believe that 100 percent of the U.S. population—that's right, every single one of us—have traces of these toxins in our bodies. Thirty-seven percent of us suffer from chemical sensitivities, skin rashes, and allergies, many of them provoked by the chemicals in our cleaning products.

Breaking It Down

Health Effects of Toxins

It's important to understand the different types of problems exposure to these chemicals can provoke. Some reactions are *acute*, meaning we feel the effects immediately: our eyes water, we break out in a rash, or we begin coughing or sneezing uncontrollably.

Other health effects can be *chronic*, or long-term: hormonal problems, developmental and learning disabilities, the buildup of fluid in the lungs, even cancer. Asthma and arthritis are both examples of chronic health problems.

The EPA has classified many of the chemicals found in household cleaning products as *persistent bioaccumulative toxins,* or PBTs. The term "persistent" refers to the length of time that a chemical compound stays in the environment, once introduced. A compound may persist for less than a second or indefinitely, for tens or thousands of years.

A bioaccumulative substance is one that increases in concentration in living organisms over time. When toxins bioaccumulate in the fatty tissues of our bodies and enter the food chain, they can cause serious long-term health problems and even alter our genetic makeup permanently. The EPA defines persistent bioaccumulative pollutants as "chemicals that are toxic, persist in the environment and bioaccumulate in food chains and, thus, pose risks to human health and ecosystems. The biggest concerns about PBTs are that they transfer rather easily among air, water, and land, and span boundaries of programs, geography, and generations."

Many toxic substances do not readily *biodegrade*, meaning they cannot easily be broken down by other living organisms. Readily biodegradable substances quickly decompose into harmless by-products, while an "inherently" biodegradable substance will biodegrade eventually.

It's the nonbiodegradable substances that cause the real problems.

In landfills, nonbiodegradable trash decomposes *anaerobically*, or without oxygen, a process that releases harmful *methane* by-products into the atmosphere and greatly contributes to global warming. (In humans, cancer cells feed on anaerobic activity, while healthy cells feed on oxygenated, aerobic activity.) Nonbiodegradable chemicals don't just persist in our ecosystem. They also hang around for a long time inside our bodies, where they contribute to numerous health problems that worsen over time.

Associated Problems in Humans

The chemicals found in conventional cleaning products can affect a great variety of our body systems.

• A neurotoxin is any poisonous chemical that acts on the body's brain and nervous system. Neurotoxins, which can affect cognitive function, have been linked to lower IQs in children. Known neurotoxins are found in some air fresheners, disinfectants, spot removers, and permanent-press fabrics. Other known neurotoxins are mercury and manganese.

• A carcinogen is any substance that can cause or aggravate cancer. Many of the chemicals found in popular cleaning products—all-purpose cleaners, dishwashing liquids, furniture polish, oven cleaners, glass and window cleaners, air fresheners, spray starch, flea and roach bombs, and spot removers—have known or suspected carcinogenic properties. (For a list of chemicals known to cause cancer in humans that are found in household cleaning products, please see the Glossary of Chemicals on page 203.)

• A mutagen is any agent that causes a permanent genetic change in a cell. The term *mutagenicity* refers to the capacity of a chemical or physical agent to bring about this unnatural permanent alteration. Phenol, an ingredient in many spray starches, laundry detergents, all-purpose cleaners, air fresheners, disinfectants, and furniture polish, is both a mutagen and a suspected carcinogen.

• Endocrine disrupters can be naturally occurring hormones or man-made chemicals that may interfere with the body's hormonal or reproductive system. Endocrine disrupters can mimic, block, or interfere with natural hormones, causing all sorts of problems to develop, including altered immune function, developmental disabilities, and endometriosis. Some laundry detergents, furniture waxes, and metal polishes might contain endocrine disrupters, which can also be referred to as hormone mimics, hormone disrupters, or reproductive disrupters.

• Teratogens are substances that interfere with fetal development, causing malformation or serious deviation from normal development of embryos and fetuses. Some glass cleaners, all-purpose cleaners, and spray starches might contain teratogens.

Protecting Our Children

Why do I keep putting such a big emphasis on our children? Well, for a number of reasons, children are the most vulnerable to environmental insults. Several behavioral and biological factors make children exceptionally sensitive to chemical exposures:

• Children are like sponges, absorbing everything, both good and bad, in the environment around them. They're smaller than adults, and are constantly growing. They breathe faster, taking in more air—and more chemicals—relative to their weight than we do.

• Young children wash their hands less frequently than adults and often put their hands and foreign objects in their mouths, which means they have direct contact with the chemicals we use to clean their homes.

• Because they are shorter than adults and spend more time on the floor, children are more directly exposed to chemicals like chlorine, which are heavier than air and lie closer to the ground.

• Children have accelerated metabolisms. They consume far more food and drink than the average adult per pound of bodyweight—roughly three to four times as much.

• Rapid growth and splitting of cells during childhood allows dangerous cell mutations to multiply at a faster rate.

• Small children, because they are unable to read the warning labels on household cleaning products, are likelier to spill or swallow products left around the house.

• A newborn's skin is more permeable and more readily absorbs chemicals. These exposures can have lifelong consequences.

I guarantee that there are even more risks to children that we don't even know about yet, since most environmental exposure standards have been set up according to research conducted on adults—180-pound males, to be precise. By definition, then, the Food and Drug Administration current safety standards and regulations fail to take most children, pets, and even adult women into account.

Researchers have cited difficulties in obtaining informed consent and getting blood samples from children. As a result, children—the population that should be the centerpiece of these studies—often get overlooked.

There are other problems, too, in measuring the health impact of these toxins on children. Because there's often a long delay, called a "latency period," between chemical exposures and the diseases they cause, researchers cannot always determine clear-cut associations. But even without all the answers in yet, it's obvious that children's health is in a state of crisis. We're seeing epidemic levels of asthma, diabetes, learning disorders, and obesity. Pediatric cancers are on the rise. One in every six kids is diagnosed with a learning disability or other developmental issue, from dyslexia to ADHD to bipolar disorder. Childhood allergies are at record levels, and juvenile rheumatoid arthritis has become the third most common chronic disorder.

We can, and must, work harder to protect our children from the diseases that are ravaging them. A 2003 report by the National Institute of Environmental Health Sciences states that "prevention of exposure is the single most effective means of protection against environmental threats." Until all the facts are in, we need to protect our kids by limiting their exposure to these dangerous chemicals. They're getting sicker, and they need our help.

Health Problems Associated with Environmental Toxins in the Home

These toxins are causing numerous problems in our children, everything from headaches to pediatric cancer. Here is a list, by no means comprehensive, of the childhood health issues with known or suspected links to chemical exposures:

ADHD
Allergies
Asthma
Autism
Blurred vision
Cancer
Chemical sensitivities
Coma
Convulsions
Cough
Cramps
Developmental delays
Diabetes
Diarrhea
Disturbances in liver function
Dizziness
Drowsiness
Dry mucous membranes
Dry skin
Elevated blood pressure
Endocrine disorders
Fatigue

Fever, flu-like symptoms
Genetic damage
Headache
Heart rate changes
Hoarseness
Hyperactivity
Immune system problems
Irritated eyes, nose, throat,
    skin
Joint pain
Loss of coordination
Lower IQ
Memory loss
Motor skills impairment
Nausea and vomiting
Nervous system damage
Neurodevelopmental disorders
Reproductive problems
Respiratory paralysis
Seizures
Tightness in the chest
Tremors

Asthma

We can see the impact of these environmental exposures in the rising asthma rates in this country. Overall, asthma rates have nearly doubled in the last twenty years. Between 1980 and 1994, the prevalence of asthma increased 75 percent overall and 74 percent among children between the ages of five and fourteen.

Asthma is now the most common chronic childhood illness, affecting nearly 5 million people under the age of eighteen. Today, approximately one in thirteen schoolchildren suffers from asthma. It's the leading cause of emergency-room visits and missed school, blamed for 6 percent of absenteeism overall. In Canada and the United States, five children die from asthma every week.

Asthma is caused by a genetic predisposition, but we need to start asking why so many people have this predisposition these days. Asthma can also be triggered by respiratory irritants in the environment: It's no coincidence that low-income and inner-city populations have the highest rates of childhood asthma. There might also be a link between asthma and obesity, which is also at epidemic levels in the United States.

Developmental Disorders

Exposure to environmental pollutants can also lead to neurological impairments and a wide range of developmental delays. Though scientists have only recently started tracking the relationship between chemical exposures and developmental delays, studies suggest that children exposed to these chemicals are at a greater risk of dropping out of school, becoming pregnant as teenagers, abusing drugs, committing crimes, becoming institutionalized, even committing suicide. These problems damage not only the afflicted children but their parents and siblings and teachers. They weaken entire communities.

One in every 166 kids born today is diagnosed with some form of autism spectrum disorder (ASD)—a number that has increased nearly tenfold over the past decade, according to the August 2003 *Journal of Autism and Developmental Disorders*. Roughly 25,000 children are diagnosed with autism every year, or 1 out of every 104 boys, whose autism rates are four times higher than girls'.

Rates of attention deficit and hyperactivity disorder (ADHD) are also at record highs: In the past decade alone, we have seen a sixfold increase in ADHD diagnoses, with an estimated 8 million American children taking Ritalin.

Childhood Cancer

This year, 570,000 Americans will die from cancer. Approximately 2,300 of these victims will be children and adolescents, making cancer the leading cause of disease-related death among children between the ages of one and fifteen. Between 1975 and 1998, childhood cancer rates in the United States increased approximately 21 percent, or a rate of about 1 percent a year. (We will not know the current statistics until the World Health Organization and the National Institutes of Health release the results of their next comprehensive survey later in the decade.)

Researchers at the University of Massachusetts at Lowell and the Boston University School of Public Health have linked these steadily increasing cancer rates to various environmental contaminants: car emissions, pesticides, and parents' exposures to the toxins commonly found in paints and petroleum-based solvents. Many of these exposures take place before birth—the toxic substances can cross the placenta and damage the developing fetus—or even prior to conception, particularly if parents work in a heavily polluted environment.

The National Cancer Institute estimates that childhood cancer will continue to increase at a rate of 1 percent annually, especially cases of acute lymphoblastic leukemia (ALL) and brain tumors in children age five and under. According to the American Cancer Society, approximately 16,000 American adults and children are diagnosed with a brain tumor every year. But as usual, it's our kids who are suffering the most: The average onset of brain tumors occurs between the ages of five and ten. The average onset of ALL, the most common pediatric cancer, is usually between the ages of three and five.

While it's extremely difficult to isolate the exact environmental causes of childhood cancer, we know that the disease results from many interconnected variables involving both genetics and the environment. Lifestyle factors such as exposure to secondhand smoke and a poor diet—and overexposure to toxic substances—might play a big role in incidences of childhood cancer. Researchers have found a direct link between the development of childhood leukemia in children whose parents were occupationally exposed to pesticides or petroleum solvents. Other small studies have implicated pesticides in cases of non-Hodgkin's lymphoma and brain tumors as well. In 2002, experts at Mount Sinai Hospital concluded that only 10 to 20 percent of childhood cancers could be attributed solely to genetic predisposition. The remaining 80 to 90 percent of all pediatric cancer cases are at least partially caused by lifestyle and environmental factors. The World Health Organization, concurring with these findings, has found that cancer and many other devastating diseases can mostly be prevented.

It's true that every year, more and more children survive cancer. Mortality rates have decreased significantly over the past two decades. ALL has a 75 to 80 percent chance of being treated successfully, and overall, 70 to 75 percent of children diagnosed and treated for cancer within the last twenty years are still alive.

Despite this encouraging news, we need to do more than improve survival rates. We must also work to eliminate the causes of cancer, since even successfully treated childhood cancers can give rise to a host of other serious health problems later in life. Children treated for leukemia, for example, have a higher risk of developing malignant brain tumors or other cancers as adults.

Birth Defects

What role do toxins play in the growing number of birth defects in this country? We can't yet say with certainty. About 2 to 3 percent of babies born today have a major birth defect, and roughly 18 percent of newborns are diagnosed with some minor structural anomaly, but we still don't know exactly what role the environment plays in these problems. Scientists have only recently begun studying the links between birth defects and chemical exposures, and several complicating factors need to be taken into account as well. Sometimes a fetus can come into contact with an endocrine-disrupting chemical while still in the womb, but the consequences might not show up until years later.

We're still not exactly sure at what age the critical exposure takes place, or precisely what role the environment plays in birth defects: A recent estimate put environmental factors anywhere between 3 percent and 25 percent. But no one can dispute that children are born today with a shocking concentration of toxins in their bodies. "Body Burden: The Pollution in Newborns," a landmark 2004 study by the Environmental Working Group, found that some industrial chemicals can enter our systems before we're even born.

The Body Burden study included a groundbreaking investigation of the chemicals and pollutants found in newborns' umbilical cord blood. Their findings are horrifying: Of the 413 chemicals tested for, 287 of them were present in the babies' cord blood. Among the lethal toxins found: perfluorochemicals, or PFCs (found in Teflon and Scotchgard); polybrominated diphenyl ethers, or PBDEs (flame retardants used in the manufacturing of furniture foam, computers, and televisions); metals (lead, mercury, arsenic), and chlorinated dioxins.

These toxins attack every part of our bodies: our nervous, cardiovascular, hormonal, reproductive, respiratory, immune, and digestive systems; our skin, kidneys, liver, hearing, and vision. Fully 134 of these chemicals—that's just about half—are known or suspected carcinogens. More than 10 percent of women of childbearing age have levels of mercury that exceed EPA guidelines. High doses of prenatal exposure can cause mental retardation, seizures, cerebral palsy, and vision, hearing, and sensory problems. A fetus may come into contact with an endocrine-disrupting chemical while still in the womb, but associated problems—infertility, birth defects, learning disabilities—might not become apparent until later. According to researchers at UCLA, in a study published in the *Journal of American Epidemiology,* women exposed to high levels of ozone and carbon monoxide in urban areas have a greater chance of giving birth to babies with serious heart defects.

Understanding Indoor Air Pollution

When talking about air pollution, most of us think in terms of outdoor air quality. But did you know that air pollution might be two to five times worse indoors than out? In fact, the EPA consistently ranks indoor air quality among the top five environmental risks to human health. Polluted indoor air can also reduce our ability to perform mental tasks that require concentration, calculation, or memory.

Because we spend roughly 90 percent of our time indoors, we are constantly exposing ourselves to pollutants inside our homes, schools, and workplaces. Indoor air contains dust mites, bacteria, and asthma-inducing allergies; particles from cooking, cleaning, smoking, and pet dander; and pollutants brought in from outdoors like pollen, pesticides, and heavy metals. These particles, many of which are known or suspected carcinogens, are often more concentrated inside than outside the house. The reason for this? Air outside is constantly circulating, while indoor air is stagnant and trapped. Poor ventilation, wall-to-wall carpeting, and other factors can make it even harder for polluted air to escape outside.

According to the WHO, indoor air pollution is responsible for 1.6 million deaths a year—that's one death every twenty seconds! For the past seven years, the EPA has ranked indoor air pollution as one of the top five risks to public health. Contaminants in the air have been linked to pregnancy loss, reduced birth weight, SIDS, acute respiratory infection (ARI), respiratory symptoms, reduced lung function, asthma, cancer, and neurocognitive function.

But despite these risks, we haven't yet developed universal standards for what constitutes a "healthy" indoor environment. While the Clean Air Act and other laws legislate standards for outdoor air quality, we alone control the quality of the air inside our homes. We need to act immediately to reduce our indoor air pollution, because as usual, it has a disproportionately severe effect on children. One in five schools in America has indoor air quality issues, and allergic reactions to "sick" indoor air environments keep ten thousand American children out of school every day. Dust-mite allergies, thought to afflict roughly 10 percent of the U.S. population, can lead to asthma in susceptible children.

Indoor air quality is an issue that affects all of us. Many of us have heard about the risks of lead paint and asbestos in older construction, but did you know that even new, modern homes can seriously harm our respiratory systems? A WHO study conducted in 1984 indicates that up to 30 percent of all new and remodeled buildings contain contaminated air in some form. There is even a medical term for this phenomenon: sick building syndrome (SBS).

If you're concerned about your home's indoor air quality, you can call the EPA's Indoor Air Quality Information Clearinghouse (IAQ INFO) toll-free at 800-438-4318 during regular business hours Monday through Friday. You can also ask questions by fax (703-356-5386), e-mail (iaqinfo@aol.com), or mail:

Indoor Air Quality Information Clearinghouse (IAQ INFO)
P.O. Box 37133
Washington, DC 20013-7133

In the next chapter, I'll be offering many concrete suggestions for improving your indoor air quality. In the meantime, you should be aware that chemical cleaning products play a big role in indoor air pollution.

The Science of Housekeeping

To make informed decisions about which cleaning products to use, you first need a basic understanding of how and why they work.

A Brief History of Soap

We humans have been cleaning ourselves for as long as we've been around on Earth. Thousands of years ago—the first known soaplike substance, in ancient Babylon, dates back to 2800 BCE—people made soap by boiling fats with ashes. The ancient Egyptians bathed, treated diseases, and even styled their hair with a soap made from animal fats, vegetable oils, and salts. Later still, the Romans constructed gorgeous bathhouses that elevated personal cleanliness into an art form.

By the Middle Ages, a decline in personal hygiene played a big part in the fourteenth-century plague that wiped out a huge portion of the European population. By the time cleanliness came back into vogue, in the seventeenth century, people all over the continent had been manufacturing soap for centuries, but until the nineteenth century, soap, which was heavily taxed, was a luxury few ordinary people could afford.

Around the same time, in the late eighteenth and nineteenth centuries, several chemists made important discoveries central to the modern science of soap making. The first of these, in 1791, involved turning salt into soda ash, or sodium carbonate, which combines with fat to make soap. As other discoveries advanced soap-making technology, factories started producing soap cheaply and in vast quantities. By the middle of the nineteenth century, the soap-making industry was among the fastest-growing in America. Soap was no longer a luxury item, but an everyday necessity. Various formulas were created for different functions—milder ones for bathing, stronger ones for the washing machines that became available at the beginning of the last century.

Soap-making technology didn't change much until World War I, when a widespread shortage of the animal fats used for soap prompted chemists in Germany to develop the first known detergents. Detergents, unlike traditional soaps, are "synthesized," or derived from synthetic materials. The production of household detergents—initially used for hand dishwashing and the laundering of delicate fabrics—took off in this country in the 1930s.

Another big breakthrough took place right after World War II, with the introduction of the first "built" detergent: a formula that combined surfactants, the main cleaning agent, with "builders," which boosted the cleaning power of the surfactants. Within ten years, Americans were buying more detergent than soap. Over the next decades, manufacturers introduced more and more synthetic detergents to the market, and the relentless production hasn't stopped since. The following list tracks the major advances in household cleaning products over the past half century:

1950s
- Automatic-dishwasher powders
- Liquid laundry, hand-dishwashing, and all-purpose cleaning products
- Liquid fabric softeners
- Detergent with oxygen bleach

1960s
- Prewash soil and stain removers
- Laundry powders with enzymes
- Enzyme presoaks

1970s

- Liquid hand soaps
- Dryer-sheet fabric softeners
- Multifunctional products (e.g., detergent with fabric softener)

1980s

- Detergents for cooler water washing
- Automatic dishwasher liquids
- Concentrated laundry powders

1990s

- "Ultra"—or superconcentrated—powder and liquid detergents
- Ultra fabric softeners
- Automatic dishwasher gels
- Laundry and cleaning-product refills

Most of us cannot imagine life without these heavy-duty chemical cleaners. But it's useful to remember that it was only in the second half of the last century that these chemical products that we now take for granted first came into existence. I'm obviously not suggesting that we return to prehistoric soap-making techniques. I just want to remind everyone that there are alternatives to the chemical cleaning products developed over the last fifty years, products that we now know have done us more harm than good.

Some Basic Terms

Surfactant: A surfactant reduces the surface tension of water so that it can spread more easily over a surface. In other words, surfactants—the basic ingredient of most laundry and dishwashing detergents—make water "wetter."

Surfactants can be either plant-based or petroleum-based. I recommend only purchasing products with vegetable-based surfactants, which are for the most part derived from coconut, soy, or corn. Long-term exposure to petroleum-based surfactants can have neurotoxic and carcinogenic effects. Surfactants fall into three basic categories: (1) detergents, (2) wetting agents, and (3) emulsifiers.

Builder: A builder is an additive that increases the cleansing action of soaps and detergents. Before the EPA banned their use in laundry detergents, phosphates were the most popular builders.

Solvent: Solvents, substances in which other substances are dissolved, prevent the separation of ingredients in liquid cleaning products, dissolve organic soils, and clean without leaving a residue. Unfortunately, many chemical solvents can be extremely dangerous to humans. Solvents commonly found in household cleaning products include naphtha (in bathroom floor cleaners and metal cleaners), ethanol (in hand dishwashing liquids and carpet cleaners), and propylene glycol (in many personal-care products). There are several different types of solvents:

• Petrochemical solvents—including methylbenzene and toluene (found in some furniture polishes)—are colorless flammable liquids that have been linked to cancer and other serious illnesses.

• Chlorinated solvents—including methylene chloride (found in some air fresheners), TCA (found in some spot removers and furniture waxes), and PERC (found in some spot removers and dry-cleaning fluids)—are organic solvents composed of chlorine atoms. These strong respiratory irritants are huge environmental contaminants.

• Volatile organic compounds (VOCs) are substances that contain carbon and different proportions of other elements such as hydrogen, oxygen, fluorine, bromine, sulfur, or nitrogen. VOCs become vapors and gases at room temperature, and we easily absorb them into our bodies.

Aerosol Propellant: An aerosol propellant is a compressed inert gas that works to discharge the contents of an aerosol container. Propellants—including isobutene, butane, propane, and hydrocarbon compounds—are found in carpet cleaners, air fresheners, and many other products. These eye, throat, and respiratory irritants can aggravate asthma and cause other lung diseases. Exposure to propellants can also lead to eye injuries and chemical burns. If you can possibly help it, avoid aerosol products, which deplete the ozone layer.

Bleaches: Bleaches whiten and brighten fabrics, and also help remove stubborn stains. They convert soils into colorless, soluble particles that can be removed by detergents and carried away in the wash water. Avoid chlorine bleach, which can destroy your clothes in the process of disinfecting and deodorizing them. Oxygen bleach—sometimes referred to as "color-safe" bleach—is far gentler and effectively cleans most washable fabrics. It's also much better for your health.

Preservatives: Preservatives slow the aging and decay of a product. The most famous and widely used preservative, formaldehyde, is a known carcinogen in humans.

Antimicrobial Agents: Antimicrobial, or antibacterial, agents kill or inhibit the growth of bacteria and other microorganisms that can cause diseases. Unfortunately, many chemical antimicrobial agents, also known as germicides or tuberculocidals, kill the good organisms along with the bad. Popular antimicrobial products also frequently contain triclosan, a common disinfectant that the American Medical Association is urging the FDA to regulate more closely. Throughout the book, I will be giving you many alternatives to chemical germicides.

Different Shades of Green

When I first started cleaning up my life over twenty years ago, I had to search for days to find even a fraction of the environmentally friendly household products that are now being sold in even the smaller grocery stores. The few environmentally conscious corporations that did exist back then—Ecover started in 1980; Seventh Generation and Bi-O-Kleen were both founded in 1988—still catered exclusively to specialty customers.

But these days, it's getting hip to be green. The resources are improving all the time for ecoconscious consumers. Unfortunately, as the toxic companies become aware of the growing demand for healthier cleaning alternatives, they've decided to cash in on the trend—though without actually getting rid of the toxins. They're advertising "natural" air fresheners and "lavender-scented" fabric softeners. But what does "natural" really mean? Is the lavender scent derived from an actual lavender plant, or is it synthetic, and how can anyone know the difference?

In most cases, these labels are just another tactic to lure consumers. These companies are probably hoping that we won't ask too many questions or find out that they're still using the dirt-cheap synthetic raw materials that compromise the integrity of their formulas, just to save a little money on the manufacturing end. Because this industry is so unregulated, companies can claim that their products are "nontoxic" or "environmentally friendly" when all they've done is remove the ammonia, say, or the chlorine bleach, from the formula. Many of these so-called "green" products still contain toxins like propylene glycol or benzene or petroleum-based synthetic fragrance. These companies haven't stopped using toxic synthetic chemicals in their formulas.

This is why you should always exercise extreme caution when shopping for cleaning products. The people who market these products are so, so clever, even educated consumers need to be constantly on guard. Don't be fooled by clever marketing tricks. Not all green products are created equal. There are different levels of organic and different levels of green. Taking out some of the chemicals is not good enough. We should only accept products with the lowest level of toxicity possible. One good rule of thumb is this: Whenever the option exists, only buy products that disclose all ingredients. I don't think companies should be forced to give their whole formulas away. Of course not; that's what makes their products unique. I'm just saying they should list the ingredients. A mother should be able to look at the back of a window-cleaner bottle and find out exactly what's in that product. She should be able to determine if ingredients are synthetic or vegetable-based, toxic or naturally derived.

At my center, we're pushing for legislation that makes companies define what exactly is in their products, and what impact those ingredients will have on human health. One day, every single cleaning product on the market will meet the following guidelines:

- Full disclosure of all ingredients
- Third-party certification of product formulations
- Rigorous quality assurance/quality control program
- A purified water supply that is free of chlorine and residual chlorine
- Required certification of raw materials by suppliers

- Product formulations that meet or exceed established American Society for Testing and Materials (ASTM) standards for the specific product category for efficacy
- The least level of toxicity possible while maintaining the highest level of efficacy
- Must be cost competitive with traditional cleaners

Slowly, the laws are starting to change to make these proposed requirements a reality. In food packaging, for example, the "USDA Organic" label must now be followed by an asterisk and exact specifications of which ingredients are organic. Products can no longer be advertised as "organic" or "natural" without any substantiation.

But the cleaning-products industry is still lagging behind. There are still *no* universal standards for household cleaning products. The nonprofit organization Green Seal (http://greenseal.org/), which certifies the "environmental responsibility" of a whole range of consumer goods, has to this date only set standards for *institutional* cleaning products. Even these are completely inadequate and fail to provide our children the level of protection they deserve. Though meant to designate the environmental safety of a product, the Green Seal standards still permit ingredients that may seriously harm human health. They also

- Do not stipulate the use of natural or naturally derived ingredients
- Allow for petroleum-derived ingredients
- Do not adequately address ingredients that may be potential carcinogens, teratogens, mutagens, or endocrine and hormone disrupters
- Allow for synthetic fragrances
- Allow for chlorinated organics

- Do not address the potential bioaccumulation of certain chemicals
- Do not call for disclosure of all ingredients
- Lack provisions for product safety
- Allow for phosphates

These days, we know way too much to keep defaulting to these anti-quated standards. Many schools and hospitals have already adopted criteria that protect the health of our children without compromising product efficacy and incurring additional costs. The law should, too.

The Tier System

Consumers everywhere need to learn that cleaning products can be different degrees, or shades, of green. At my center, we've established rigorous standards for the ingredients in our products, adapted from the U.S. Department of the Interior's "Guidance and Training on Greening Your Janitorial Business." We've also developed a tier system for product standards that we believe should be adopted nationally. To be labeled "green" or "ecofriendly" or "child safe," products must first meet universal requirements. Those that pass certain minimum criteria should then be assigned to one of three categories: Tier I, Tier II, or Tier III.

Tier I: Tier I cleaning products—the greenest of the green—should meet the following standards:

- Must be free of any known or suspected human carcinogens, mutagens, teratogens, and endocrine disrupters.

- Must not contain nonylphenol ethoxylate (NPE) or alkylphenol ethoxylate (APE).

- Must not contain compounds or substances that cause or contribute to the creation of atmospheric greenhouse gases, ground-level smog, or ozone depletion.

- Must not be corrosive to skin or inanimate surfaces.

- Must not be a severe skin or eye irritant.

- Must not be delivered in single-use aerosol cans or cans using ozone-depleting propellants.

- Must not contain petroleum-derived or petrochemical blended fragrances.

- Must not contain heavy metals that are toxic to humans, animal life, or the environment.

- Should not be combustible below 150° Fahrenheit.

- Must not contain chlorine or chlorinated or brominated solvents.

- Must not contain compounds that persist or bioaccumulate in human or animal tissue or in the environment.

- Must not contain volatile organic compounds (VOCs) at levels exceeding the limits established by the Southern California Air Quality Management District Resources Board for the applicable product categories. Products must not be on the Environmental Protection Agency's list of hazardous air pollutants.

- Should be readily biodegradable at greater than 90 percent in thirty days without needing to be run through a municipal effluent treatment process. If not biodegradable due to inorganic content, the ingredient must be chemically inert.

- Must be obtained or derived from replenishable natural (plant) sources.

- Should be derived from renewable resources.

- Should be as concentrated as possible to green the supply chain. Products should be capable of being dispensed through automatic systems in order to reduce user and environmental contact.

- Should have a pH level between 4 and 10 whenever possible.

Tier II: Tier II products are a little less green, but still pretty good. Tier II products contain ingredients that are to the greatest extent possible natural or naturally derived, but might also include some synthetic ingredients for which effective natural or naturally derived alternatives have yet to be developed. To be certified as Tier II, products should meet these standards:

- Should contain to the fullest extent possible natural or naturally derived ingredients.

- Should contain synthetic ingredients only if naturally derived alternatives are not available, and only to achieve and maintain the desired efficacy.

- Should achieve a neutral pH whenever possible.

- Should contain low or no VOCs whenever possible.

- Should be derived from renewable (plant) resources whenever possible.

- Must not contain heavy metals that are toxic to humans, animal life, or the environment.

- Must not be delivered in single-use aerosol cans or cans using ozone-depleting propellants.

- Must not contain ozone-depleting ingredients or phosphates.

- Must not contain nonylphenol ethoxylate (NPE) or alkylphenol ethoxylate (APE).

Tier III: Products in Tier III, while containing ingredients that are to the greatest extent possible natural or naturally derived, may also contain some synthetic ingredients for which natural substitutes have yet to be developed. Most "green" sanitizers and disinfectants will fall into this category, at least until researchers conclusively establish that natural products can kill germs as effectively as synthetic micro-biocides. To the fullest extent possible, Tier III products should meet the following standards:

- Must contain surfactants that are naturally derived from renewable resources.

- Must not contain heavy metals that are toxic to humans, animal life, or the environment.

- Must not be delivered in single-use aerosol cans or cans using ozone-depleting propellants.

- Must not contain nonylphenol ethoxylate (NPE) or alkylphenol ethoxylate (APE).

- Must not contain ozone-depleting ingredients or phosphates.

- Must achieve a neutral pH whenever possible.

- Should use synthetic ingredients only if naturally derived alternatives are not available, and only to achieve and maintain the desired efficacy.

Eventually, my center hopes to establish a national procurement protocol for these standards. There need to be laws dictating the information that should be disclosed on the labels of household products. Until that happens, arm yourself with information so that you can make the best choices for your family. Education is the key weapon in the battle for our children's health. The more we know, the more we can protect them.

Toxic Interruption
Petroleum Distillates

We're crazy for oil, can't get through a minute of the day without it. We depend on petroleum for absolutely everything—not just to run our cars and heat our homes, but to scent our bodies and polish our furniture and wash our dishes. Petroleum and its by-products are found in a staggering variety of consumer products: lip gloss, perfume, hand dishwashing liquid, fertilizer, pesticides, plastics, paint thinners, solvents, motor oil, and fuels. Almost all artificial fragrances are petroleum based.

Petroleum is a thick natural oil that consists of various hydrocarbons, or chemicals that contain both hydrogen and carbon. The term "petroleum distillates"—which can be used interchangeably with "petroleum derivates," "petrochemicals," "hydrocarbons," and "naphthas"—refers to a broad range of chemicals that are extracted during the petroleum-refining process.

Whenever possible, avoid these potential toxins. They can be detrimental both to the environment and to your health. Petroleum distillates—including propane, butane, and toluene—are dangerous neurotoxins that have been linked to serious reproductive disorders and blood poisoning. These highly flammable bioaccumulative compounds smother the skin and also pose risks to the liver and the respiratory, cardiovascular, immune, endocrine, and gastrointestinal systems. And according to a study conducted at the University of Massachusetts at Lowell, children with acute nonlymphocytic leukemia (ANLL) were 2.4 times likelier to have parents who were exposed to petroleum products on their jobs.

Given these hazards—and the prevalence of petroleum distillates in our everyday lives—you might logically assume that the manufacturers of petroleum-based consumer goods would thoroughly test their products for safety on human health. Unbelievably, this is not the case. There's still a lot we don't know about petroleum distillates.

Some measures have been taken to keep these poisons out of the hands of our children—the Poison Prevention Packaging Act (PPPA) of 1970 requires child-resistant packaging for some products with petroleum distillates or other hydrocarbons—but we have a long way to go. In the European Union, laws severely restrict the use of petroleum distillates in the manufacture of cosmetic products. In this country, all we've done is to ban petroleum distillates from food products, and that's not good enough.

A Petroleum Distillate by Any Other Name . . .

Mineral oil, or liquid petrolatum, is a by-product of the distillation of petroleum in the gasoline-production process. Because this chemically inert, transparent, colorless oil is so cheap to produce in large quantities, the personal-care, automotive, and cleaning-products industries all make use of this refined-petroleum distillate. While the least refined mineral oils, such as those used by the automotive industry, may be carcinogenic, the toxicity of the highly refined mineral oils used by the cosmetics and cleaning-products industries is still undetermined. Even so, until the facts are in, I'd try to avoid floor soaps and wood polishes that contain mineral oil.

two:
one change at a time

Chapter 4

The Home

Nesting

I've always been fascinated by how birds build their nests, by how resourceful they are in gathering materials for their homes. In Manhattan, I've watched them construct their homes out of drinking straws, candy-bar wrappers, and plastic baggies. The birds that nest at the ranch in New Mexico use more traditional building materials: adobe, mud, and sticks. On the Connecticut coast, I've seen birds make their nests out of seaweed and shells.

But even if their selection of materials depends on their habitat, birds are extremely careful about what they bring into their nests. They build their nests to protect their children, to increase their chances of survival and safeguard them from harm. And in this respect, we're not all that different from birds. Our nests also reflect the choices we've made, the type of environment we've created for ourselves. Wherever we're living—in a trailer, subdivision, apartment, or mansion—we all take pride in our homes. And no matter what they're made of—wood, brick, stone, adobe, metal, plastic, or concrete—our homes are the place where we feel most comfortable in the world, where we store our possessions and make our memories.

Our nests should also be places of healing for our families. Let's start taking better care of them, so that our loved ones can thrive. Throughout the next chapters, I'll be giving you advice on how to clean every part of your house: the kitchen, bathroom, bedroom, living room, and laundry area. I'll be teaching you how to use a few simple nontoxic products to clean your tiles, your counters, your tubs, and your sinks. I'll also be telling you which products you'll need for this project—I guarantee it's fewer than you think. But before getting into the nitty-gritty of cleaning, I wanted to offer some basic guidelines that you can apply to every room of your house.

Some Cautionary Notes

Reading Labels

Check the label of your trusty furniture polish and try finding out exactly what's in it. Or your spray glass cleaner, or tile scrub. More often than not, you'll come up short of information. This is no accident on the part of the companies that make these familiar products. The law does not require cleaning-product manufacturers to list ingredients that make up less than 0.1 percent of listed carcinogens or 1 percent of listed OSHA chemicals. The labels of most conventional household cleaners list only "active" ingredients and omit listing the "inactive" or "inert" ingredients, even those that are potentially harmful. In many cases, these unspecified chemicals can make up as much as 98 percent of the product. A good rule of thumb is: If the label is incomplete, chances are there's something in that product that you don't want to be inhaling or ingesting.

Food companies and shampoo makers have to list their ingredients—why shouldn't the manufacturers of cleaning products? Both end up in our bodies and bloodstream. Most conventional cleaning products contain a mixture of chemicals, including potential carcinogens, neurotoxins, teratogens, mutagens, endocrine disrupters, and hormone mimics. Many of the 287 synthetic chemicals that the Body Burden study found in umbilical cord blood probably entered the mother's system through fabric softeners, carpet protectors, and wood varnishes. And yet the cleaning-products industry remains completely unregulated. We're never even told how dangerous these all too familiar substances can be.

It's insane that the laws haven't changed yet. The manufacturers of all consumer goods should be required to disclose the ingredients clearly on the labels, so that people can see what exactly they're allowing into their homes.

The Hidden Dangers of Product Packaging

When shopping for cleaning products, you should always look at the bottom of the bottle to determine which type of plastic you are buying.

Plastics are ranked on a scale of 1 to 7. If possible, stick to #1 and #2 plastics, which are the least toxic and the most widely recycled. Avoid plastics labeled #3, which contain PVCs (see page 116). PVC, more popularly known as vinyl, is made from the carcinogen vinyl chloride and releases an even more powerful carcinogen, dioxin, during the manufacturing process. Because very few municipal recycling plants accept #3 plastics, most PVCs are doomed to pile up on the landfill and emit poisonous gases into the environment. Plastics numbered 4 through 6 are soft plastics and can degrade into your food and enter your bodies, so I'd avoid those as well. Get more information from the Green Guide; Spokane Regional Solid Waste System, www.solidwaste.org/reccodes.htm.

Artificial Fragrances

Toiletries, cosmetics, air fresheners, cleaning products, and many other consumer goods are packed full of artificial fragrances. On any given label, the word "fragrance" can refer to as many as six hundred different chemicals used in the formula. Here again, the makers of these products keep the specific ingredients a secret from the public. The manufacturer would probably claim that this is to protect trade secrets, but the fact is that if more of us knew the truth about artificially scented products, we'd immediately stop buying them.

Some artificial fragrances are used to create a pleasant odor, others to disguise the odor of other, less appealing chemicals. In fact, even some products identified as "unscented" or "fragrance free" contain a synthetic masking fragrance formulated with many of the same toxins. These misleading labels are unacceptable in light of what we're beginning to learn about the impact of artificial fragrances on human health.

The National Institute for Occupational Safety and Health has found that fully one-third of the substances used in the fragrance industry are toxic. According to "Neurotoxins: At Home and the Workplace, Report by the Committee on Science and Technology, U.S. House of Representatives," 95 percent of chemicals used in fragrances are synthetic compounds derived from petroleum.

For some time now, we've known that fragrance ingredients can severely irritate the skin. They can also be allergens, photosensitizers, and phototoxins. But in more recent years, studies have shown that fragrances can damage more than just the skin. They can also cause headaches, sneezing, and watery eyes. Some chemicals used in fragrances, like methylene chloride, are carcinogenic. Many artificial fragrances also contain the carcinogenic preservative formaldehyde, which can enter the body through various routes, wreaking havoc even at low levels of exposure.

With our increased exposure to artificial fragrances, clinical accounts have shown a corresponding increase in fragranced products causing, triggering, and exacerbating existing health conditions. Fragrances can induce or worsen respiratory illnesses, particularly in people already afflicted by asthma, allergies, sinus problems, rhinitis, and other conditions. Acetylethyltetramethyltetralin (AETT) and musk ambrette, two common materials used in fragrances, can exhibit neurotoxic properties, meaning they can damage the brain and central nervous system.

Animal studies have indicated that AETT caused a bluish discoloration of internal organs. Similar studies have indicated that musk ambrette was readily absorbed through the skin and also exhibited potential neurotoxic properties. While there are relatively few studies available regarding short-term and long-term exposure, experts are getting concerned about the respiratory, neurological, and systemic problems that might result from bioaccumulation of these toxins in the food chain.

Considering how relentlessly we're assaulted by them, it's crazy how little health and safety data we have about the raw materials used in fragrances. For now, the best thing we can do for our health is to limit our exposure to these dangerous chemical compounds by buying only products scented with all-natural essential oils or other botanically derived fragrances.

Finding the Right Natural Alternatives

What if there are no natural alternatives? In most cases, there are. You just might need to be a little creative about tracking them down. Be resourceful. Do a search on the Internet, ask someone at your local health food store, or just start experimenting on your own with baking soda and vinegar and other natural cleaning agents that I'll be discussing later in the chapter. Remember that less is more—in general, we use way too many products. Most of the time, we simply don't need these chemicals that are polluting our bodies! When it comes to disinfecting and sanitizing, for example, the simplest solutions are usually the most effective: No chlorine bleach or triclosan-tainted antibacterial soap does a better job of disinfecting than old-fashioned distilled white vinegar, and the essential oil of oregano has proven natural antibacterial and antimicrobial properties as well.

What if natural alternatives do exist, but not near my home? I admit that there can be real obstacles to obtaining many of these natural cleaning products. Out at the ranch, the closest big natural foods store to us is in Santa Fe, which is an hour's drive away. There's a smaller health food store in Las Vegas, New Mexico, a half hour away, but even that's way too far to drive just for a bottle of glass cleaner. It's just not reasonable to expect a mom to spare the time or gas for such a minor errand.

People living in many other parts of the country are in the same situation: they can either go to their neighborhood mom-and-pop store that sells the usual toxic cleaning products, or they can go to Wal-Mart. When it comes to green cleaning products, the selection can be limited to nonexistent.

Luckily, it's getting easier every day. I really do believe that there's a green cleaning revolution on the horizon in this country. More human-friendly cleaning products are becoming available all the time. Still, while Wal-Mart and some of the other big-box stores are beginning to stock environmentally responsible cleaning alternatives, we're not all the way there yet. It can still be difficult to find nontoxic alternatives outside major metropolitan areas.

Together, we can change that. If your local grocery store carries only the toxic brands, try speaking with the floor manager and suggesting that he order some of these nontoxic alternatives. Never forget that retailers exist for no other reason than to serve the needs of their customers. If enough individuals request nontoxic cleaning products, the store will eventually stock them.

Trust me: These methods work. The whole organic food movement got started in this country through this kind of grassroots petitioning.

Moms asked their local stores to start carrying organic food and some-times even got a petition circulating in the community. Once the stores understood that they could sell the organic food, they wasted no time in stocking it. As long as retailers can make a profit, they'll supply the goods.

If we all work together, we can ignite the same movement with non-toxic cleaning products. As consumers, we have the ultimate power—let's start using it for our children's good.

But until that happens, you can order most of the products I'm rec-ommending over the phone or on the Internet. Buy in bulk, and you'll save on both shipping costs and the product itself. You can also start greening your cleaning by incorporating common household ingredients like baking soda and distilled white vinegar into your routine.

Improving Your Indoor Air Quality

As I discuss in the previous chapter, toxins in the air are more dangerous indoors than out. Because they are trapped in enclosed spaces, the chemicals in our homes are unusually concentrated. They have a very di-rect impact on our quality of life. Indoor air contaminants have been linked to pregnancy loss, reduced birth weight, SIDS (sudden infant death syndrome), respiratory symptoms, asthma, cancer, and learning disabilities—and probably more problems that haven't yet been studied.

The good news is, in addition to boycotting chemical household cleaners, we can take other simple steps to improve the air quality of our homes. The more toxins we can eliminate, the healthier we'll be.

Houseplants

A number of houseplants can absorb dangerous toxins in the air includ-ing benzene, PVCs, carbon monoxide, nitrous oxide, and formaldehyde, according to a recent two-year study by NASA and the Associated Landscape Contractors of America. Plants not only boost oxygen levels; in some conditions, they can remove up to 87 percent of toxins from the air! Houseplants don't cost much, and they look great.

While almost any plant can improve the indoor air quality of your home, philodendrons, green spider plants, dracaenas, palms, ferns, English ivy, peace lilies, mums, and daisies have been shown to be the most effective at reducing gaseous pollutants in the air. These plants don't require much light, so you can put them in every room of your house— you'll immediately notice a big difference.

But do be advised that houseplants also add moisture to the environment. Avoid overwatering the plants, particularly if you already have a problem with mold or mildew.

If you live in a densely populated urban area, or on a street with heavy traffic, you should also consider a pine plant or tree. Pine is known for its amazing ability to absorb vehicle emissions, carbon dioxide, and other industrial pollutants. I have pine trees all around my terrace in New York to give my family that one extra layer of protection from the toxins in our environment.

HEPA Filters

High efficiency particulate air (HEPA) filters remove particles from the air at a minimum efficiency rate of 99.7 percent. While they can help reduce dust, mold spores, and other allergens, they're less effective than plants at removing gaseous pollutants, particularly carbon monoxide. HEPA filters come in a variety of sizes. You can purchase plug-in room units, or have filters installed in your central air-conditioning. If you have allergies, experts recommend vacuuming every day with a HEPA vacuum. Whatever HEPA filter you choose, you must maintain and replace the filters on a regular basis, as they become much less effective when clogged.

Rock-Salt Lamps

When we come back from the beach, we feel clean, refreshed, renewed. That's because most of us who live in cities are deficient in negative ions, and the clean, sunny sea air restores them to us. To achieve this sensation more than a couple of times a year, try getting a rock-salt lamp.

Rock-salt lamps are *negative ion generators,* which give us back the negative ions our urban environments lack. Negative ion generators, which come in a variety of forms, use static electricity to generate negative ions that kill organisms like dust, odors, allergens, mold, mildew, smoke, fungi, dust mites, pet dander, bacteria, and pollen in our environment. I recommend rock-salt lamps in particular because they create an attractive glow and give off ample light, and they're much safer than ozone generators. If you have a problem with mold, dampness, or mildew, they can also help remove humidity from the air.

Essential Oils

I can't praise essential oils enough. At home, I use them constantly to purify and scent the air. I'm addicted! Why use toxic artificial fragrances when these natural air fresheners work so much better? When placed in a cold diffuser, essential oils can eat up odors from cooking, mold, mildew, airborne microorganisms, and other everyday pollutants that enter the home.

Some essential oils have powerful disinfecting properties as well: The pressed oils of oregano, basil, clove, and thyme in particular are highly antimicrobial, antibacterial, and anti-inflammatory. Oregano, thyme, and rosewood oils have been proven to destroy strep pneumonia cells. In 2001, a researcher at Georgetown University did a study showing that the essential oil of oregano—or specifically carvacrol, a main chemical component in oregano—can combat dangerous bacteria and treat infection as effectively as antibiotics. The next year, two orthopedic surgeons on different continents reported that the oils of Eucalyptus radiata and Melaleuca alternifolia (better known as tea tree) often work better than modern antibiotics at treating certain infections. And in 2004, British researchers at the University of Manchester found that essential oils could destroy the MRSA "Super Bug" bacteria responsible for hospital-acquired infections, and prevent approximately five thousand deaths a year.

And beyond all of those benefits, essential oils just make your home a more nurturing, welcoming place to be. When I first walk into the house, I diffuse all sorts of different oils: rosemary, grapefruit, lavender, sage, lemongrass, frankincense, cedar, lemon, orange, tangerine; a blend of clove, cinnamon, and eucalyptus. You can buy preblended oils, or just experiment with combinations on your own. I buy most of my oils at www.youngliving.com. They're so pure, you can actually ingest most of them.

There are literally hundred of different oils that you can choose from, and as you begin to combine them, you'll develop your own personal preferences. Ask at your local health food store for therapeutic Grade A oils, and remember, a few drops go a long way. Through the holidays and winter, I like to diffuse Dr. Young's Christmas Spirit blend of orange, clove, and cinnamon.

Dehumidifiers/Humidifiers

People in the Southwest should use humidifiers to prevent excessive dryness. On the East Coast, in the South, and in other wet, swampy climates, I recommend using a dehumidifier to minimize the levels of moisture in your indoor environment. Dehumidifiers prevent mold and mildew and purify the air. For natural deodorizing, you can add essential oils such as lemon, grapefruit, sage, cedar, clove, and frankincense to your humidifier or vaporizer to scent the air. As always, follow manufacturer's instructions, and be sure to test the oil in the vaporizer or humidifier first by placing a dab on a small test area that will not affect the performance of the machine. Some essential oils can damage the plastic parts.

Air-Conditioning and Heating Units

Central air-conditioning units, which keep the air circulating throughout the whole house, tend to be better at controlling indoor air quality than window units. You can install HEPA filters in your AC units, but be sure to change them regularly, or however often the manufacturer recommends. You should also consider getting an AC unit with some form of humidity control. The ideal humidity level of a room is 24 percent.

Back to the Basics

Essential Cleaning Products

Now that we've gone over these simple principles, I want you to go look under your kitchen sink, or inside your utility closet, or wherever you keep your household cleaning products. You probably have a lot of different bottles stashed away—most Americans do.

So, what did you find in there? Window/glass cleaner, toilet-bowl cleaner, spray bleach, detergent, fabric softener, dryer sheets, spot remover, spray starch, automatic dishwashing detergent, hand dishwashing liquid, furniture polish, oven cleaner, scouring cream, shower cleaner, tub and tile cleaner, carpet shampoo, and probably several other products you can no longer remember why you bought in the first place.

When we greened Hackensack University Medical Center, the janitorial staff had been using twenty-two different cleaning products. This inflated figure was pretty typical of the hospitals and other institutions—including schools—that we visited. Some places were using up to twenty-five or thirty different products. By the end of the greening process at Hackensack, we'd cut that number down to eight core and eleven total, half of what they used to order.

Like hospitals, we waste a great deal of money and precious storage space on specialty products. You actually only need a handful of versatile nontoxic products to clean your entire house.

- **All-purpose cleaner** for floors, counters, kitchen surfaces, bathrooms, tubs, tiles, carpets, spills, and stains

- **Window/glass cleaner** for glass, windows, and all stainless steel

- **Automatic dishwashing detergent**

- **Hand dishwashing liquid** for pots, pans, dishes, fine china, glasses, teapots, coffeepots, silver, and anything else you don't want to put in your dishwasher

- **Laundry liquid**

- **Baking soda,** or sodium bicarbonate, is unbelievably useful in every room of your house. It can neutralize acid, scrub shiny materials without scratching, unclog and clean drains, extinguish grease fires, and remove certain stains. Baking soda can also be used to deodorize your refrigerator, carpets, and upholstery. It can clean and polish aluminum, chrome, jewelry, plastic, porcelain, silver, stainless steel, copper, and tin.

- **Distilled white vinegar** works much better than any toxic disinfectant you can buy. It contains about 5 percent acetic acid, which makes it great at removing stains. Vinegar can also dissolve mineral deposits and grease, remove traces of soap, remove mildew or wax buildup, polish some metals, and deodorize almost every room of your house. You can use it to clean coffeepots, windows, brick, stone, carpets, toilet bowls—just about every surface in your house except marble, in fact. A tablespoon of white vinegar added to the rinse cycle also acts as a wonderful fabric softener. While it's normally diluted with water, in some cases, it can be used straight. I recommend using organic vinegar, which is slightly pricier than the nonorganic kind but still a lot cheaper than most consumer cleaning products.

- Lemon juice is a natural odor-eater that combines well with other ingredients. It can be used to clean glass and remove stains from aluminum, copper, clothing, and porcelain, and nothing works better on Formica surfaces. If used with sunlight, lemon juice is a mild lightener or bleach. Squeeze the juice from half a lemon into the wash cycle to get rid of odors on clothing.

- Table salt is great at removing rust. With lemon juice, it can clean copper. When mixed with vinegar, salt polishes brass. Salt is also a key ingredient in an effective, all-natural scouring powder.

- Hydrogen peroxide can be diluted to remove stains from heavily soiled whites and other clothing and a number of surfaces. You can dip a cotton swab in diluted hydrogen peroxide to remove stains from thick white curtains.

- Essential oils

- Ketchup can be used to clean copper and brass.

The Supply Closet

To do any job properly, you need the right tools. Just as a carpenter needs hammers and nails, and an artist needs paints and brushes, we all need good equipment to clean our homes. We also need to give a little more thought to how we organize and care for our household cleaning supplies. I've seen it over and over again at the hospitals and schools we've greened—administrators lose a ton of time and money because they've never bothered to develop an efficient cleaning protocol.

A little preliminary organization will go a long way toward boosting the efficiency—and the enjoyment—of your household cleaning routine. Instead of buying more and more "new and improved" cleaning products, take stock of the ones you already own. Wherever you keep your cleaning supplies—in a closet, on a shelf, or underneath the kitchen sink—that space should be organized, clean, and welcoming. In the long run, you'll save yourself a lot of time and money.

For the same reasons, you should also learn how to use your cleaning supplies properly. We break more irons and vacuum cleaners because we've never bothered to read through the instructions than for any other reason. I always recommend investing, if it's possible, in really good equipment, and then learning how to use and maintain that equipment. Try to get the best iron—if you can. Try to get the best vacuum cleaner—if you can. Then, teach yourself how to use your equipment correctly so that it will last.

> *"My mother has no interest in the environment or global warming or any of that other 'nonsense' (her term). What she does have: severe allergies and respiratory problems. Still, she's very attached to her tried-and-true toxic cleaners—until I sent her a package of nontoxic alternatives for Mother's Day a few years ago. She couldn't believe how well they worked! She's since gotten rid of all the synthetic chemical cleaners—again, not because she be-*

lieves they have an impact on the world around her, but because
they get her home clean better than anything else. And not
coughing or choking as she scrubs is a great side effect, too."

Jane M., Houston, TX

In maintaining your supplies, you'll also be doing your part for the
environment. Take the following example: Say your iron breaks because
you've been filling it with tap instead of distilled water. Because getting
such a small appliance fixed is usually more trouble than it's worth, you
end up throwing that iron away. Once in the landfill, that iron will release
mercury, lead, cadmium, and other heavy metals into the atmosphere.
The end result: You've wasted money and contributed to our global
warming problem. Wouldn't it make more sense just to read the instruc-
tion manual?

Essential supplies:

1. Cleaning products (see list above)

2. Microfiber mop

3. Sponge mop

4. Washable microfiber cloths: You can buy several different
kinds of microfiber cloths. We use one to clean televisions, plasma
screens, and computer monitors. Another cleans wood finishes, while a
third cleans glass and mirrors. There is no end to the usefulness of these
cloths.

5. Steel wool/scouring pads: Avoid pads with toxic detergents
in them. You can add hand dishwashing liquid as needed. Use steel wool
sparingly, as it can scratch surfaces.

6. Natural cellulose sponges: Sponges are bacteria traps, so be sure to replace often. If you use a kitchen sponge for too long, you'll be spreading bacteria all over your kitchen. I suggest buying a bulk package and changing them every five days.

7. Nonchlorine-bleach recycled paper towels

8. Vacuum cleaner with a HEPA filter

9. Hand microfiber duster: You'll need one with a long handle/ extension to reach ceilings, fans, delicate light fixtures, and other high corners. You'll also need a smaller duster for more basic everyday dusting.

10. Iron and ironing board

11. Rags, yellowed old T-shirts, or bar towels: The Lifekind catalog (www.lifekind.com) sells certified organic cotton kitchen towels.

12. Buckets: I love keeping a stainless steel bucket in my laundry room to soak soiled clothes in overnight. They're affordable and last forever. But because stainless steel buckets are too heavy to lug around and can also scratch floors, I use regular plastic buckets for cleaning and mopping.

13. Old toothbrushes: Toothbrushes, with a little baking soda and lemon juice, are great for scouring. They work on clothing, bathroom tiles, rugs, linens, and tablecloths, among many other uses. Be sure never to use a toothbrush from the kitchen in the bathroom or vice versa— keep toothbrushes for different purposes neatly separated. When you're done using the toothbrush, soak it for ten minutes or so in vinegar or

dip it in a little hydrogen peroxide to kill bacteria. If you take this precaution regularly, you can use the same cleaning toothbrush for up to six
months.

14. **Large scrub brush:** You can use this in the bathroom, on tub
surfaces and tiles, instead of harsh scouring products.

15. **Gloves:** Gloves are useful both for doing dishes and for cooking and serving food to large groups of people.

For information on where to obtain these supplies, refer to p. 193 in
the Resources section.

Spotlight on: All-purpose Cleaners

In simplifying the way you clean, it's important to have a really great all-
purpose cleaner that you can use to clean countertops, floors, sinks, toi-
lets, tubs, and even clothing stains. Unfortunately, most conventional
all-purpose cleaners are a mixture of potentially dangerous chemicals.
Contrary to popular opinion, we absolutely don't need these toxic formulas to disinfect our homes.

All-purpose cleaners contain many potentially hazardous chemicals we should go out of our way to avoid. Some of these toxins are endocrine disrupters and hormone mimics. Others can cause nausea,
respiratory problems, kidney and liver damage, even cancer.*

---

*For detailed information on these toxins, please refer to the Glossary of Chemicals on
p. 203, as well as the alkylphenolic compounds Toxic Interruption on p. 181, the butyl
cellosolve Toxic Interruption on p. 156, the chlorine bleach Toxic Interruption on p. 24,
and the phenols Toxic Interruption on p. 144.

These products may contain:
- Alkylphenolic compounds
- Artificial fragrances: see also p. 65
- Butyl cellosolve
- Chlorine bleach
- Diethanolamine (DEA)
- D-limonene
- Morpholine
- Organic solvents
- Phenols
- Triethanolamine (TEA)
- Trisodium phosphate can irritate the skin, eyes, nose, and throat. Contact with eyes can lead to conjunctivitis, while ingestion can injure the mouth, throat, and gastrointestinal tract. Breathing the dust of trisodium phosphate may aggravate asthma or other chronic pulmonary diseases.

Suggested Natural Alternatives: There are lots of excellent nontoxic all-purpose cleaners out there. And because they are more concentrated than their toxic counterparts, they last much longer. My Imus GTC product line has an excellent all-purpose cleaner that we use in every room of the house. Bi-O-Kleen, Ecover, Seventh Generation, Earth Friendly, Sun & Earth, and other green companies all make this core product as well.

Disinfecting Naturally

Disinfectants—which, depending on their specific function, are sometimes called "bacteriacides" or "germicides" as well—have one simple and utterly essential purpose: to annihilate the bacteria, microbes, and germs that cause disease. All-purpose cleaners described as "antibacterial" or "antimicrobial" have been formulated with this goal in mind as well. Doctors and hospital workers rely on disinfectants for their ability to prevent the spread of all sorts of different infections: tuberculosis, salmonella, E. coli, various fungi, herpes simplex, the common cold, even diarrhea.

Unfortunately, most disinfectants on the market today are formulated from a blend of toxic, caustic chemicals: from synthetic pine oil to chlorine bleach and ammonia. These products might kill all the bad germs on any given surface, but they also wipe out the good microorganisms that boost our immune systems and keep us healthy and balanced.

When we greened Hackensack University Medical Center, we got the janitorial staff to cut down from twenty-two cleaning products to eight core and eleven total. Of these, only one contains toxins, and that's the germicide used in operating rooms to prevent the spread of infectious diseases. We couldn't provide a nontoxic germicide because in this country, hospitals and nursing homes are required by law use a germicide officially registered as a tuberculocidal, or a substance that has been proven to kill the tuberculosis bacillus. Right now, all registered tuberculocidals are highly toxic. Despite scientists' efforts to establish the effectiveness of natural germicides like oregano, the FDA—for various political reasons—probably won't approve them for many years to come. These restrictions might prove dangerous in the end, as new strains of bacteria emerge that resist these synthetic chemicals.

In your home, you should immediately replace your synthetic disinfectant with a nontoxic all-purpose cleaner. Any all-purpose cleaner with essential oils has natural antibacterial, antimicrobial, disinfecting properties, and of course vinegar is also a great disinfectant.

Flooring

Carpeted Floors

If you have any choice in the matter, opt for less carpet and eliminate wall-to-wall carpeting whenever possible. Carpet in the kitchen and bathroom is particularly ill-advised, because fabrics absorb toxins in the air and are much more difficult to clean. Because carpet retains dampness more than other types of flooring, it can worsen preexisting mold and mildew problems.

Unless your carpets are made from organic fabrics and vegetable dyes, they may be petroleum-based, emit volatile organic compounds (VOCs), or contain toxins such as formaldehyde and xylene, both of which contribute to indoor air pollution. I will cover the dangers of toxic carpet cleaners and natural ways to clean carpet in Chapter 7, *The Bedroom*.

Noncarpeted Floors

Most other floors in our house are made of linoleum, wood, brick, vinyl, ceramic or stone tile, cork, or bamboo. Most of these surfaces can be cleaned using the same methods, without resorting to harsh chemical products that strip our floors.

✳️ **The Importance of Dry Mopping:** It isn't necessary to wet-mop as often as most of us think. Though the frequency of your floor-cleaning regimen often depends on the foot traffic through your house, once or twice a week is usually enough. We're addicted to using products for even the simplest household chores, but most of the time, dry mopping and vacuuming will achieve the same effect. I don't, however, recommend sweeping too often—dirt can get trapped in the broom and circulate around your house. I just keep a small, handheld broom for minor clean-ups and spills.

Mopping Up

For your really heavy-duty cleaning, add a nontoxic all-purpose cleaner and/or distilled white vinegar to warm water. Mop as usual to clean gummy, greasy substances off your floor. You definitely don't want to use the vinegar solution every time you mop, though. It can be really harsh and can even strip some wood floors. Instead, you should alternate it with a good nontoxic all-purpose cleaner. For your regular everyday cleaning, I recommend using a nontoxic all-purpose cleaner diluted with water. Follow these guidelines to get the cleanest floor with the least amount of work:

1. Always dust mop or sweep floor before mopping.

2. Use a putty knife to pick up any gum or debris that has adhered to the floor. If you don't have a putty knife, an old butter knife will work just as well.

3. Use the proper dilution of either concentrated cleaner or white vinegar. (Too much of a product may affect the floor finish and its appearance—you don't want to damage your floor permanently while attempting to clean it.)

4. Always "cut in" (mop floor edges and corners keeping mop parallel to the wall). This eliminates splashing the walls and controls dirty build-up in the corners

5. Mop the floor in a figure eight pattern, always overlapping your strokes.

6. Keep the heel of the mop on the floor.

7. Use both sides of the mop.

Mopping Tips

- Every other time you mop, alternate between a vinegar-and-water solution and an all-purpose cleaner.

- Change your solution often. Dirty water will not clean your floor.

- Clean mop bucket, wringer, and mop head after every use.

- And remember, you probably don't have to wet mop as often as you think. Try dry mopping, vacuuming, and sweeping more often to achieve the same level of clean with fewer products.

※ Essential Oil Tip: Add a quarter cup of vinegar to a bucket of warm water. Then mix in five to ten drops of an oil of your choice, or try the antibacterial blend (lemon, clover, grapefruit, tangerine, sage, and spruce).

Choosing the Right Mop

Dry Mopping

- For the best results, I recommend a microfiber mop. You can throw the microfiber cloths that attach to the mop head in the washer and dryer and use each one between five and ten times.

Wet Mopping

- For wet mopping, I'd go with a regular sponge mop with a replaceable head—these are the easiest mops to rinse and clean. Switch out the sponge head every eight weeks, or after no more than eight uses, to avoid excessive bacteria buildup.

- Traditional white string mops tend to collect mold and bacteria. They just have too many nooks and crannies to keep clean—bacteria and dirt can build up after just a few uses.

• Steer clear of the premoistened disposable mop cloths. These no-fuss instruments have become incredibly popular over the past few years, and no wonder: they appeal both to our laziness as a culture and to our inexhaustible passion for new products. But be careful, because the premoistened mopping pads might contain triclosan or chlorine bleach, which are both chemicals that you should avoid.

※ Product Recommendations and Purchasing Information: Microfiber Unlimited, Inc., makes a cleaning wand set that "is not pretreated with any chemicals."

> *"After years of mopping my clothing boutique with pine cleaner, I got tired of the strong chemical smell that lingered for hours afterward and sometimes even lingered on the fabrics of the clothes on the rack. On a whim I bought a nontoxic all-purpose cleaner, and the rest is history. My store smelled fresh and clean—no more airing it out for the rest of the evening. I was so impressed that I took the cleaner home and now use it for absolutely everything."*
>
> *Sarah M., Bolinas, CA*

Toxic Interruption
Dioxin and Triclosan

Beware of dioxin: it's the most powerful animal carcinogen ever tested. A chemical by-product of paper bleaching, trash incineration, and other industrial processes, dioxin—which the EPA has been testing rigorously since 1985—is probably the most harmful man-made substance in exis-

tence. Dioxins, the name for a family of seventy-five different organochlorine chemicals, have been conclusively linked not only to cancer, but
to many other serious medical problems as well, including severe weight
loss, liver and kidney problems, birth defects, reproductive problems in
adults, deformities and developmental disorders in children, immune-
system damage, endometriosis, respiratory problems, skin disorders, and
diabetes. In some instances, dioxin can even cause death. And what's
most frightening is that dioxin can produce these effects at much lower
exposure levels than most other hazardous chemicals.

Our primary exposure to dioxin is in food, especially in high-fat
meat and dairy products, since the chemicals released by bleaching
paper and burning trash end up in the grass and soil that cows and other
animals eat, thereby entering the food chain. Like us, these animals store
dioxin and other bioaccumulative substances in their milk and their fat.
When we eat dioxin-contaminated animals, the chemical lodges in our
fatty tissues as well. In fact, the vast majority of Americans have measur-
able levels of dioxins in their bodies, and every day, most of us consume
300 to 600 times more than the EPA's "safe" dose. And because dioxins
don't readily biodegrade, these poisonous chemicals steadily build up in
our bodies over the generations.

Now we are finding that we may be creating more dioxin through
our cleaning products. Soaps, microfiber mops and cloths labeled "antibacterial" or "antimicrobial," and countless other consumer goods—from
dish and laundry detergents to mouthwashes, deodorants, cutting
boards, and sponges—frequently contain triclosan, a common disinfectant that sunlight can convert to dioxin, according to research conducted
at the University of Minnesota. The researchers found that triclosan
initially produces a relatively benign form of dioxin, but the chemical
can become much more toxic when it enters our water systems and
combines with the chlorine in there. Another big problem with triclosan,

which the EPA has listed as a pesticide, is that some germs can mutate and develop a resistance to it.

I recommend using microfiber cloths, especially for dusting and polishing furniture. They are an efficient, economical way to clean your house without overdoing it on the products. But when choosing which microfiber products to buy, you need to make absolutely sure that the fibers have no triclosan or other synthetic chemicals woven in. As usual, it can be hard to tell the difference just from reading the label.

Triclosan Alternatives
You don't need a chemical to disinfect your home. Try using essential oils with natural antibacterial and antimicrobial properties instead, like lemon, cinnamon, clove, thyme, juniper, sage, spruce, lemongrass, and grapefruit. Look for an all-purpose cleaner that contains at least two or three of these essential oils.

Chapter 5

The Kitchen

Eating In

I've always thought of the kitchen as the warmest, most welcoming room in the house—the center of gravity where we gather for meals and snacks and laid-back conversations. Because we spend so much time in there, we go to great lengths to ensure that our kitchens are sanitary and safe. But ironically enough, in trying to keep a clean kitchen, we may be exposing ourselves and our loved ones to toxins. Often, we end up ingesting traces of many of the synthetic chemicals that we use to clean our dishes and countertops and cutting boards. These chemicals may react with our food and enter our bodies, accumulating in our bloodstream, organs, and fatty tissue.

Think about it: If you wash a plate with a toxic chemical detergent and it isn't rinsed thoroughly afterward, a residue might remain on that plate long after you put it back in the cabinet. So the next time you use that plate, you might also be eating toxins along with your hamburger or salad.

I encourage you, for the safety of the people you love, to rethink the way that you clean your kitchen.

The Kitchen Sink

You can use the easy instructions that follow to clean sinks in your kitchen and any other room of your house. As usual, it's easier—and more affordable—than you might expect.

Types of Sink

• Copper and brass: To clean copper and brass sinks and tubs, all you need is salt, warm water, and some lemon juice. Using a cloth, soft sponge, or rag, start rubbing down the copper sink with a mixture of salt and water. Because these two ingredients combined can be somewhat abrasive, you should add lemon juice as you go along. As you wipe it down, the whole surface of the sink will be transformed before your very eyes, turning shiny and clean. After rinsing off the cleaning solution with cold water, wipe the sink completely dry. This step is crucial, because as soon as water gets on copper, the surface will start to blacken again. The key is to keep the sink dry when you're not using it. You can also clean copper and brass by squirting some ketchup on a cloth and rubbing it over the surface of the metal. It works wonderfully!

• Acrylic and porcelain enamel: Make a paste out of nontoxic hand dishwashing liquid and baking soda. Once a thick paste forms— that's the texture you want—just wipe the porcelain enamel sink with a cloth and scrub it. Avoid using salt on a porcelain sink; it can be abrasive and start to wear down the enamel. If your porcelain or acrylic sinks have a tendency to turn yellow, just saturate some kitchen cloths with distilled white vinegar and lay them on the inside surface of the sink for a couple of hours. You'll get the same effect as with chlorine bleach, minus the toxins.

- **Stainless steel:** If your sink is stainless steel, just squirt a little hand dishwashing liquid on a cloth or sponge, add water until it gets soapy, and rub down the surface. Once you've done that, spray on some nontoxic glass cleaner and go over the surface again to get rid of any smudges from the soap. Towel-dry to prevent water marks.

Faucets

To clean your faucet—whether it's stainless steel, brass, acrylic, or has a brushed or shiny nickel finish—you can use the same method I'm recommending for stainless steel: Just rub it down with nontoxic hand dishwashing liquid or nontoxic all-purpose cleaner and water, then buff it to a shine with some nontoxic glass cleaner and a microfiber cloth.

Drains

On the edge of some sinks and bathtubs, you'll occasionally notice caulking or a black residue around the drain cover. To prevent your sink from looking corroded or rusted, you never need to use chlorine bleach. Instead, just make a thick paste using lemon juice, a little salt, and baking soda. Spread the paste over the blackened, grimy surface and let it sit for as long as it's convenient: at least an hour, or all day if you work outside the home. Because the solution is completely natural and noncorrosive, you don't have to sit around with a timer, waiting to wash it off—for most busy moms, that just isn't a practical solution. Whenever you get home, just rinse off the paste. You'll be amazed by how shiny and clean your drain looks!

To get rid of lingering odors in your sink, make a paste of baking soda, vinegar, and a little lemon juice. Once again, just let this paste sit for however long you need. The paste will not only take away the odor, but a lot of the rusty residue as well. Repeat this procedure when necessary—it really depends on how often you use your kitchen sink. In

New York, my family cooks several times a day, so we make this paste every week or two. If you don't eat at home that often, you might only need to treat your drain every couple of months.

✳ **Cleaning Stainless Steel:** Most traditional stainless steel cleaners are extremely toxic, loaded with suspected neurotoxins and carcinogens. They often come in combustible, nonbiodegradable cans, too, and contain aerosol propellants that irritate the respiratory system.

When we were greening hospitals—which, along with schools, workplaces, and airports, have stainless steel absolutely everywhere—we managed to eliminate these dangerous products completely.

To clean stainless steel, just put a little hand dishwashing liquid on a cloth or scouring sponge, add water, and wipe down whatever surface you're trying to clean. Once you've gotten rid of the dirt and grease in this way, use a nontoxic glass cleaner to remove any smudges or marks that might remain. This method will work to clean and polish ovens, stovetops, refrigerators, and any other stainless steel appliances in your kitchen, including refrigerators.

> *"My nontoxic glass cleaner is far more versatile than the chemical spray cleaner I used for so many years. I spray it on all my stainless steel kitchen appliances and even inside my microwave with terrific results. I also use it on my granite countertop—that, too, looks better than ever. There's no longer any risk of streaking, clouding, discoloring—or poisoning! I love that."*
>
> *Jordis R., Minnetonka, MN*

Countertops

You should never use toxins on the surfaces where you prepare food—
you're clearly risking contaminating it. It's just not worth it, when a combination of simple ingredients will work just as well to keep your kitchen
counters clean and germ free.

Types of Countertop

- **Acrylic:** Acrylic countertops are easy to clean. Just rub down with
hand dishwashing liquid and warm soapy water. You can follow with a
squirt of vinegar to disinfect this durable material.

- **Ceramic tile:** A lot of Spanish-style, Southwestern-style, and
tropical-style homes have tiled countertops with grout in between. You
can clean these surfaces with hand dishwashing liquid, along with vinegar every once in a while. You don't want to use vinegar too often because
it can eat up the grout between the tiles. You can also try making a paste
out of lemon juice and baking soda to take out some of the stains on the
grout.

- **Wood:** On wood countertops, as on wood flooring, you cannot
use vinegar daily; you have to alternate between it and an all-purpose
cleaner. Most of the time, you can clean wood just by rubbing a soft cloth
along the surface. A simple soap-and-water solution also works well; just
be sure that you dry it off afterward. To polish wood, I like to use the essential oil of lemon mixed with organic olive oil or linseed oil.

- **Marble:** Marble makes for a beautiful countertop, but it is also
an extremely porous substance, so it's crucial never to use vinegar or any

product that contains vinegar when cleaning it. Vinegar will ruin marble. Instead, just use a hand dishwashing liquid (one that does *not* contain vinegar), or an all-purpose cleaner to wipe the marble down.

• **Concrete:** A lot of people have concrete countertops today. They're tough and easy to clean—all it takes is some warm water and a squirt of hand dishwashing liquid or a nontoxic all-purpose cleaner on a cloth or sponge.

• **Soapstone, flagstone:** To clean these, just use hand dishwashing liquid or a nontoxic all-purpose cleaner.

• **Corian:** Corian, a synthetic material, is one of the most common countertops in hospitals. Because it is seamless, impermeable, and easy to clean, Corian countertops are becoming increasingly popular in homes across America as well. You can get Corian clean with just hand dishwashing liquid or a nontoxic all-purpose cleaner. To buff it, spray a little nontoxic glass cleaner on it—that's all you'll ever need to do.

• **Granite:** You can use an all-purpose cleaner to clean granite countertops with excellent results.

※ **Essential Oil Tip:** For cleaning surfaces, fill a large #2 plastic squirt bottle (at the ranch, we use the 32-ounce size) with distilled water and a few drops of dishwashing soap or all-purpose cleaner. Then add to this mixture three to five drops each of lemon, clove, cinnamon, and spruce essential oils. Shake the bottle until all the ingredients blend together, and you've got an extremely versatile surface cleaner for any room of your house.

Scouring

Products designed specifically for scouring are completely unnecessary. Many of them are also highly toxic and can scratch stainless steel, ceramic, and most tiles. Hand dishwashing liquid on steel wool or a scouring sponge can just as effectively get rid of rust, dried food, and other stubborn stains without the toxins. But these sponges can be abrasive, too, so on your more delicate surfaces, I'd advise just using a dishtowel and nontoxic dishwashing soap. You can also make your own natural scouring powder with water and dry table salt, or water and baking soda.

Scouring pads are also good for removing stubborn stains from your stainless steel pots and pans, but you don't want to use them on your dishware. These sponges can be too abrasive and might scratch the top glaze off your ceramic plates. Instead, soak the plates in hot soapy water and use a rubbery silicone spatula to scrape off whatever residue didn't come off in your dishwasher.

Stovetops

To get rid of really tough greasy stains on your stovetop, you don't need a harsh chemical agent that might react with the heat the next time you turn on your stove. A little hand dishwashing soap or a nontoxic all-purpose cleaner on a scouring sponge will work on your most stubborn stains.

Doing the Dishes

By Hand

Spotlight on: Hand Dishwashing Liquids

Conventional hand dishwashing liquids can be hazardous to children, so you should really think twice before bringing such a dangerous substance into your home. Some popular petroleum-based hand dishwashing liquids might contain respiratory irritants, neurotoxins, endocrine disrupters, even suspected carcinogens.*

These products may contain:
- Petroleum distillates
- Sodium hydroxide
- Sodium laureth sulfate, sodium lauryl sulfate, and other synthetic surfactants

Learning more about
Synthetic Surfactants

Hand dishwashing liquids, like many personal-care products, typically have surfactants in their formula—these so-called "sudsing" or "foaming" agents boost the efficiency of a product. But there's a big difference between natural, botanical-derived surfactants and the synthetic variety. Some synthetic surfactants do more than just make bubbles.

Diathanolamines (DEA) are slow to biodegrade, and they can react with natural nitrogen oxides and sodium nitrite pollutants in the atmosphere to form nitrosamines, a family of potent carcinogens. **Sodium laureth sulfate** and **sodium lauryl sulfate**, the core ingredients of most conventional hair shampoos, can enter the bloodstream after very limited exposure and might also be "penetration enhancers," meaning they allow other chemicals to penetrate deeper into the skin. Other synthetic surfactants, like **nonylphenol ethoxylates (NPEs)**, have estrogenic properties and can be toxic to aquatic life.

---

*For detailed information on these toxins, please refer to the Glossary of Chemicals on p. 203, as well as the petroleum distillates Toxic Interruption on p. 58.

Knowing these hazards, I use only hand dishwashing liquids with naturally derived surfactants. They're just safer, both for me and the environment.

Suggested Natural Alternatives: Today, you can choose among several great plant-based dishwashing soaps that will clean your dishes and counters without compromising your family's health. At most of the bigger grocery stores, you can find hand dishwashing liquids from Imus GTC, Bi-O-Kleen, Ecover, Seventh Generation, and other environmentally responsible companies. Why not give one of these formulas a try? You have nothing to lose and everything to gain by this simple choice.

✳ **Essential Oil Tip:** Adding a few drops of an essential oil such as spruce, lemon, bergamot, grapefruit, or tangerine to the water while you are soaking dishes will add fragrance and improve the antiseptic properties of your nontoxic dishwashing liquid. If your product already contains some of these essential oils, this step is unnecessary.

Spotlight on: Automatic Dishwashing Detergent

The chlorine in many popular automatic dishwashing detergents can combine with hot water to produce dangerous fumes. Those heat vapors go right into your lungs, and into the lungs of your pets and your kids. Automatic dishwashing detergents contain ingredients that are irritating to humans and also harmful to the environment.*

These products may contain:
- Chlorine bleach
- Phosphates

---

*For detailed information on these toxins, please refer to the Glossary of Chemicals on p. 203, as well as the chlorine bleach Toxic Interruption on p. 24.

- Polycarboxylates
- Sodium hydroxide

Learing more about
Phosphates and Phosphate Substitutes

Phosphates, or "builders," are a major water pollutant. When built up in streams and lakes, these water-softening mineral additives encourage the overgrowth of algae and other aquatic plant life, which eventually depletes the supply of oxygen in the water and leads to the death of fish and other organisms. While the use of phosphates has long since been banned in the manufacture of laundry detergents, some automatic dishwashing detergents still incorporate them into their formulas, with disastrous consequences for the environment.

Since no longer permitted to use phosphates, many laundry detergent manufacturers have switched to synthetic phosphate substitutes. Although we lack sufficient human safety data for several of these chemicals, including *EDTA* compounds and *polycarboxylates,* we do know that neither of these phosphate substitutes readily biodegrades in the environment.

Suggested Natural Alternatives: Several great earth-friendly companies—including Bi-O-Kleen, Ecover, Planet, and Seventh Generation—make effective automatic dishwashing products that are price-competitive with the leading toxic brands.

Silverware
If you store your good formal silverware in special cloths designed to protect it, you probably won't have to polish it very often—no more than

twice a year, I'd estimate, depending on how often you use it. You can even get a drawer lined with this cloth to keep your silverware from oxidizing and tarnishing. Usually, I just rub our silverware clean with one of these cloths and maybe a little soap and water. When on the rare occasions I do use a specialty product, I generally find Weiman Silver Polish to be the most benign. But be warned that Weiman's is *not* completely nontoxic: It contains petroleum distillates. Unfortunately, I've yet to find a nontoxic product that works as well.

Pots and Pans

First off, I *never* use cookware treated with Teflon or any other "miraculous" innovation in nonstick technology. When overheated, nonstick Teflon-coated pans have been shown to release dangerous toxins into the air, toxins that have been linked to serious health problems ranging from birth defects and heart attacks to cancer. So even though its manufacturers claim that Teflon is safe unless overheated, can you really be sure you'll never let it happen? I can't. For such a minor convenience, I would never expose myself or my family to so many potential hazards—especially with all the wonderful nontoxic options out there.

Ceramic bakeware can be a nice option, although these items don't tend to last as long as other types of cookware. I love Le Creuset, which makes excellent dishes for baking casseroles and for serving meals. Le Creuset dishes are pricey, but they last forever, so it's worth investing in a few.

Other than that, the following pots and pans should work for most of your cooking:

Stainless Steel: In general, for your everyday cooking and baking, I recommend using stainless steel pots and pans with an aluminum or copper middle. All-Clad, Wolfgang Puck, and other companies make high-quality stainless steel cookware. They're safe, durable, and incredibly easy to maintain. Though expensive, they're worth the investment—collect one or two every year.

- **Cleaning stainless steel:** Fill up the pan with hot water and non-toxic soap. Boil the water down for about a minute to avoid using elbow grease. You'll be left with a pan that you can effortlessly rinse and wipe clean.

- **Making your All-Clad stainless steel cookware nonstick without toxins:** Most professional chefs already know how easy it is to make a stainless steel pan nonstick without using any chemicals. Before cooking, simply season the pan with olive oil and a couple of pinches of salt. (Note: Olive oil generally works much better than other oils for this purpose.) With the burner on medium, heat the pan and distribute the salt and oil all over the surface until it burns off. Afterward, when you begin cooking, you'll find that nothing sticks: Cleaning will be a cinch.

Cast-iron Skillet: Cooking in a cast-iron skillet can be really healthy, especially if you're a vegetarian and could stand a little extra iron in your diet. Cast-iron cookware is also really affordable, so I suggest purchasing two different sizes:

- **Multipurpose skillet:** I use my large cast-iron skillet for all sorts of different recipes. I think it's the single best tool for preparing Yukon gold potatoes, hash browns, and Texas toast—everything always comes out so delicious. But you should never cook anything too acidic, like tomatoes or tomato-based sauces, in cast iron. The acid will lift too much iron off the pan, which isn't healthy.

• Egg skillet: I have a second, smaller—about twelve-inch—cast-iron skillet that I reserve for cooking eggs. Eggs never stick to cast iron: they cook evenly, with those crispy edges I love.

• Cleaning cast iron: Instead of washing it in the sink, simply wipe it out with hot water, dry it off, then rub it down with a cloth that's been saturated in oil. I like to use a really fine organic olive oil to flavor my cast-iron skillets.

Wok: A spun-steel wok (avoid the Teflon-coated ones) is among the most versatile pieces of cookware you can own. It's the healthiest way to cook just about any food—rice, vegetables, meat, fish, tofu—because you don't have to use too much oil. In a wok, you can just braise or flash-cook veggies without running the risk of overcooking them. Slightly crunchy veggies have more nutrients, and they taste better, too.

• Cleaning a wok: You clean a wok the same way that you clean a cast-iron skillet: Wipe it down with hot water and then dry it off completely right away to prevent rusting. Then, with a cloth saturated in olive oil, wipe down the surface again. Never scrape out your wok—it will disrupt the slow seasoning process that makes food so delicious.

Copper: Copper cookware is an attractive option and a great healthy alternative. Professional cooks like to use copper because it conducts heat evenly.

• Cleaning copper pans: You can clean copper cookware the same way that you clean copper sinks and tubs: by rubbing it with warm water, salt, and lemon juice, then immediately wiping it dry. You can also clean copper with ketchup. Just rub ketchup over the surface, rinse it off with warm water, and then thoroughly wipe it dry to preserve that beautiful, shiny color.

The Importance of Drying

Dry off your copper and spun-steel pots and pans immediately after every use. If you skip this step too often, the cookware will rust and potentially become toxic. Replace any rusty pans, muffin tins, or cookie sheets in your kitchen immediately.

Toxin Spotlight
Teflon

Over the past decade, the perfluorochemicals (PFCs) used in the manufacture of Teflon-coated bakeware and other consumer products have come under intense scrutiny in the scientific and regulatory communities. Why? Because the chemicals emitted when a Teflon pan is overheated have been linked to a significant number of diseases in animals and humans.

The Environmental Working Group (EWG), a nonprofit research and advocacy organization, predicts that PFCs will one day be the single most pervasive chemical contaminant on the globe, for one big reason: they *never* biodegrade in the environment. They've done tremendous damage already. In fact, PFCs have been found to contaminate wildlife in three out of four continents tested, and one 2001 study found PFOA— the PFC in Teflon—in the blood of 96 percent of the 598 children tested across the country. To me, that's really astonishing. The Environmental Working Group found PFCs—a likely human carcinogen—in the blood of the vast majority of the U.S. population, even in the umbilical-cord

blood of newborns. Despite pressure from powerful environmental or-
ganizations, PFCs are still being foisted on the American public every day.
Even as the EPA works to get PFOAs off the market by 2015, we need to
take immediate steps to limit our exposure to these toxins that are polluting our ecosystem and endangering our children's futures.

Suggested Natural Alternatives: The French have been using silicone
bakeware for years now. At the ranch, we use little silicone placemats for
cookies, silicone muffin tins, silicone spatulas, even silicone cooking
mits. Silicone is naturally nonstick and, unlike Teflon, can withstand
high temperatures without flaking or decomposing. Silicone is easy to
wash, too—a little soapy water should do the trick. Silicone products are
increasingly available at all the places where Teflon is sold.

Cutting Boards

It's important to disinfect your cutting boards regularly, especially if
you eat meat and a lot of dairy products mixed with vegetables—
cross-contamination can lead to serious intestinal diseases. Don't take
that risk. First, you should always separate your cutting boards. If you eat
meat and dairy products, you need one cutting board for meat, one for
dairy, and a third for vegetables. You can color-code them to avoid confusion. (Obviously, if you don't eat animal products, you eliminate the need
for this sort of system.) But it is important that these food groups don't
mix before they've been cooked.

And because they come into contact with so much of our food, cutting boards should never be cleaned with chlorine bleach. Once a week,
you should soak them in vinegar after washing—it will kill the bacteria
that can cause salmonella and E. coli without any hazardous side effects.
(At the ranch, we soak our cutting boards every night because we're
preparing three meals a day for thirty people, but at home once a week
should be fine.)

• **Wood:** Avoid putting your wooden cutting board directly under running water. Too much contact with water will ruin the integrity of the wood, and the board may start to rot. Instead, immediately after prepping your food, wash the wooden cutting boards really lightly with a wet rag or sponge and some soap. Try to avoid wooden cutting boards with mineral-oil sealants. These petroleum-based coatings can be unhealthy, especially when used in the kitchen.

• **Plastic:** Plastic cutting boards are cheap, tough, and multipurpose. And unlike other kinds of cutting boards, you can just throw them into your dishwasher, where the high temperatures will disinfect them. Every night at the ranch, we soak our plastic cutting boards in distilled white vinegar for half an hour or so to kill the bacteria that might be lurking on its surface. Most of the time, you can just wash your plastic cutting board with soap and water, then rinse it off with a little white vinegar.

• **Marble:** I've said it before, and I'll say it again: Because marble is so porous, you can never use vinegar on it. Instead, just wipe your marble cutting boards down with a little nontoxic all-purpose cleaner or a little hand dishwashing liquid immediately after using. Sometimes I make a baking-soda paste to remove the tougher stains, but that's about all I ever need to keep the marble clean.

Other Kitchen Essentials

Cleaning Ovens and Other Appliances

Spotlight on: Oven Cleaners

Conventional oven cleaners are among the most corrosive of all cleaning products. When I was growing up, people I knew used to spray the entire inside of thier oven with one of those cleaners, then crank up the temperature so the toxins could work their magic. That's a pretty scary memory, now that I know about all the toxic and highly flammable ingredients in most oven cleaners. These products, which are thick enough to cling to vertical surfaces, are formulated to remove stubborn burned-on grease and other food soils from the inside of ovens.

I cannot emphasize enough that you absolutely do not need to buy a specialty product to clean your oven. Most popular aerosol oven cleaners are a dangerous blend of chemicals that can pollute the air and our lungs. Some of the ingredients might even cause cancer.* Baking soda and nontoxic dishwashing soap will get the burnt food and grease stains out of there just as effectively, with none of the health hazards.

These products may contain:
- Aerosol propellants
- Benzene
- Hydrochloric acid can dissolve and destroy tender tissues upon direct contact. Its vapors irritate the eyes, nose, and throat. Hydrochloric acid can also burn, resulting in permanent scarring and even blindness.
- Sodium Hydroxide

"When I moved into a new apartment last summer, the oven was completely disgusting—I couldn't even begin to imagine what the previous tenants had been cooking in there. I went to the store to buy oven cleaner, but all the ones they had on sale looked really frightening. Back at home I typed in 'natural oven cleaner' on Google and immediately came up with about a million

---

*For detailed information on these toxins, please refer to the Glossary of Chemicals on p. 203.

recipes for cleaning out my oven with baking soda. Unfortunately, when I gave my housekeeper the instructions, she resisted—she told me there was no way baking soda would work on that grime. But I asked her to give it a try and she eventually agreed. We were both amazed by the results—the oven was completely clean, and my kitchen didn't stink of chemicals! My housekeeper and I were both converted!"

Marianne G., New York City

Gloves in the Kitchen

For Cleaning: A housekeeper or a mother cleaning her own home might choose to wear rubber gloves for heavy-duty dishwashing jobs, like scrubbing pots and pans in hot water for hours on end. When I have a lot of dishwashing to do, I wear Cosabella latex gloves to save my hands from pruning, drying, and cracking. If you're not allergic to latex, you can try any number of kitchen gloves from Rubbermaid or other companies. Nonlatex varieties are also available.

For Food Handling: On certain occasions, you should wear gloves when serving food. If you're cooking just for your family, gloves obviously aren't necessary—just wash your hands thoroughly with nontoxic soap and hot water before and after cooking. But sometimes, if you're serving food to a large group, or cooking alongside two or three other people—when you're having a holiday party or catering an event in your home—you should take the sanitary precaution of wearing safety gloves when you prepare and serve the food. When you have several people in the kitchen chopping, prepping, and mixing, gloves help prevent the spread of E. coli and other bacteria and viruses that result from cross-contamination. At the ranch, where we're cooking three meals a day for thirty people, we always cook and serve in gloves—it saves so many problems in the long run.

You can buy at least twenty different kinds of disposable gloves for food handling, but many of them have been treated with synthetic coatings. Gloves claiming to be antibacterial might even contain triclosan, so you definitely want to avoid those. At the ranch we use Handgards (www.handgards.com) disposable food-service gloves, which are powder-free, nonallergenic, and nontoxic. They're inexpensive, so I suggest buying a case for the home.

Aprons and Other Accessories

Just as scientists wear lab coats and hospital workers wear scrubs, you should wear an extra layer over your street clothes whenever you prepare food. Wearing an apron is a no-fuss green practice that makes your kitchen more hygienic. Again, it all boils down to common sense: If you've just come inside off the street, you have soot and chemicals all over your clothes. Do you really want your kids to be digesting those particles along with their dinners? I didn't think so. Aprons safeguard your food from toxins in the environment.

The same is true for pulling back your hair when you cook or serve food: You don't want dirty, polluted hair to come into contact with the food you serve your family. Just pull it back with an elastic band and get it out of your face—nothing could be simpler.

A Word on Microwave Ovens

I don't approve of them, but if you have one and insist on using it, wipe the interior down with a nontoxic all-purpose cleaner. You can clean the front window with nontoxic window/glass cleaner.

Toxic Interruption
Ammonia

On bottles of glass and window cleaner, manufacturers boast in huge letters that their product "contains Ammonia D." I really can't believe that in this day and age, companies are still bragging about ammonia. They might as well have a skull-and-bones symbol and a message that reads, "Hey, I'm a poisonous respiratory ailment, come and buy me!" The fact that we're supposed to think ammonia's a beneficial ingredient only proves how warped and backward the whole household-cleaning-products industry has become.

Once you learn what ammonia really is, you'll never buy the stuff again. You'll know that ammonia doesn't make us cleaner—it makes us sicker. It's an extremely dangerous toxin that irritates the skin, eyes, nose, throat, and respiratory passages; repeated or high-level exposure to ammonia can lead to pneumonia, bronchitis, and pulmonary edema. The EPA lists ammonia—which has also been linked to chemical burns, cataracts, corneal damage, even skin cancer—as a toxic chemical on its Community Right-to-Know list.

Ammonia also destroys our ecosystem by poisoning plants, animals, and fish. It adds nitrogen to the environment and, like chlorine bleach, gives off vapors that can damage the deep tissue of the lungs. When used in the kitchen, ammonia makes its way into our food, and from there into our bodies and bloodstream, causing headaches, loss of sense of smell, nausea, and vomiting. People with heart conditions and asthma or other lung problems should really keep away from ammonia, which becomes even more dangerous when it reacts with other chemicals like chlorine bleach. When bleach and ammonia are mixed, they release gases that can severely damage the lungs. The toxic combination can cause tearing, respiratory tract irritation, and nausea.

Given these proven health effects, why are we still allowing ammonia into our homes? The answer is simple: because the leading manufacturers of toxic cleaning products are doing an excellent job of making it seem attractive to us.

Chapter 6

The Bathroom

Ventilation

Air quality is probably the single most overlooked and underestimated component of a healthy bathroom environment. For optimal air quality, you need to keep your bathroom ventilated at all times.

The EPA's Building Assessment Survey and Evaluation (BASE) has done several studies conclusively linking poor ventilation to bad air quality, discomfort, and numerous health problems, including Legionnaire's disease and sick building syndrome (SBS), a condition characterized by dry mucous membranes and eye, nose, and throat irritation. Typically, because they tend to be small and enclosed, bathrooms are among the worst-ventilated areas of the house, and you really don't want to breathe in too much of that chlorine smog that's released from the water system. Luckily, with just a few small adjustments, you can easily improve the ventilation of your bathrooms.

First, if you have a window in your bathroom, you should always keep it open whenever you take a shower or bath. In the summer, you'll obviously need a screen over the window to keep out the bugs. In the winter, the cooler air feels really nice and you may come to enjoy your new habit. If you don't have a window in your bathroom—and unfortunately, a lot of homes and apartments, even in suburbia, fall into this category—you can still take steps to increase the ventilation of your bathroom. Whenever you run the water and add moisture to the environment, turn on the overhead fan in your bathroom to suck up some of that toxic steam. Whenever you leave the house, especially for an extended period, leave the doors of your bathroom open to let the fresh air get in there.

Even if you have an overhead ventilation fan or a chlorine filter on your showerhead—both of which I recommend (though you need to make sure you clean your filter regularly)—you and your kids will inevitably end up inhaling the vapors of chlorinated gases. You know how your bathroom mirror fogs up after you shower? Most of that steam is toxic—a mixture of the chlorine bleach and other chlorine-based chemicals like chloroform that have been added to our water system. An open window will prevent these and other toxins, like carbon dioxide, from building up. As a general rule, the more outdoor air that circulates in a room, the safer that room is.

✳ Laundry Baskets: Always let your dirty-clothes hamper breathe a little to prevent the buildup of mold and mildew. Given the high moisture levels of most bathrooms, an open basket or hamper is preferable to a closed-off closet or cabinet—in our house, we use open wicker laundry baskets. If you do put your dirty clothes in a bathroom closet or built-in cabinet, see if there's not some way you can ventilate it—drill some holes in the top, or leave the door open an inch. Always keep wet and dry clothes separated.

Cleaning Tubs and Showers

I recently saw an ad for a new "automatic" shower cleaner that dispenses soap with the simple press of a button. Seconds later, with no effort on your part, your shower is magically clean. The product struck me as a perfect example of our obsession with over-cleaning. We're always searching for the next miraculous cleaning solution, and we'll spend any amount of money to find it—in this case, well over $20.

Obviously, no "automatic" soap dispenser can know which exact corners to clean in your shower, but that's not the only problem. You don't need to buy a separate product just for cleaning your shower—especially not one loaded with potentially toxic chemicals—and you certainly don't need to clean it every day. When we go overboard like this, we're killing all the good bacteria with the bad, and often exposing ourselves to incredibly dangerous chemicals. We've gotten into this completely out-of-control mentality in this country—as if we really believe that the more chemical products we use, the safer we'll be, even when countless studies have proved that the exact opposite is true. Really, it's all about pushing products. These companies keep coming up with new marketing ploys to trick us into wasting money every single time we go shopping. Why are we still falling for it?

We can do better than this. Green cleaning not only lowers your family's exposure to dangerous chemicals; it saves you money and simplifies your life.

> *"My son has asthma, so I always had to wait until he was out of the house to clean the bathroom—no easy task with a three year old. Even if he was at the opposite end of the house, the fumes from the toilet-bowl cleaner would cause him to cough and tear up. I was telling a friend about this problem and she suggested I start cleaning my toilet with baking soda and vinegar instead. I thought she was crazy for making such a suggestion (and told her as much!) but I had nothing to lose, so I went home and tried the recipe. I couldn't believe that it worked! Now, my son doesn't*

have to vacate the premises when I scrub out the toilet. Far from
it: he loves to watch how the baking soda and vinegar fizz when
combined!"

Kimberly, Woods Hole, MA

Dechlorinating Your Bath

Every time you take a shower or bath, you are exposing yourself—and
your family—to the chlorine used to treat 98 percent of the water systems in this country. According to the natural-products retailer Lifekind,
"Our bodies absorb ten times more chlorine during a fifteen-minute bath
or shower than they do when we drink eight glasses of chlorinated tap
water." And the total inhalation exposure of chlorine and chlorine
by-products from showering, dishwashing, and water boiling is compara-
ble to that from dietary exposure.

The hot water in your bath or shower releases chlorine fumes,
and dangerous chlorine compounds like hydrochloric acid and trihalomethanes, that accumulate invisibly in our bathrooms. Luckily, you
can easily reduce the chlorine output from your water systems. You
can purchase a dechlorinating shower filter that screws right over your
showerhead and eliminates at least 90 percent of free chlorine from
water. Several online catalogs—www.lifekind.com, www.gaiam.com,
and www.freshwatersystems.com—offer a selection of these gadgets at
reasonable prices. Lifekind and www.toolsforwellness.com also sell a
bath ball dechlorinator that you drop into the tub for a few minutes before bathing.

Cleaning Drains

In tubs and bathroom sinks, yellow, off-color rings and funky-looking
spots can form around the drains of your bathtubs and bathroom sinks.
To treat these, I use the same methods as in the kitchen. I make a paste

of salt and vinegar, or baking soda and lemon juice, and I spread it around the drain. Then, I just let it sit. If I leave the house and forget to rinse it out immediately, I never worry about it, since I know that these safe natural ingredients will not damage the surfaces of my sink and tub. Depending on your schedule, you can leave the paste sitting with towels on top for a few hours, or all day. Whenever you get back to it, just rinse off the paste first with warm water, then with cold. It's so easy to clean this way, with no extra steps or complicated maintenance involved.

To remove the black mildew some people get on the caulking in their shower, make a paste out of baking soda and lemon juice, and follow the same procedure—spot-treat the stain with the paste and leave on for as long as you need.

You can also make a paste using warm water and oxygen bleach powder. Again, just stick it on the grout and leave it on all day. Then, whenever you get a chance, rinse it off with hot water.

Cleaning Shower Curtains and Doors

Remember that the less moisture a shower curtain retains, the less mildew and bacteria will breed on it. When you leave the shower, pull the curtain open so that it can air out and dry faster—that's the key to mildew prevention. I realize, of course, that it can be hard to keep your shower curtain dry. In most busy households, by the time the shower curtain has finally dried off, someone else has turned on the shower. That's why it's important to clean your shower curtain every once in a while, particularly the liner.

Most shower curtain liners you can wash off with warm soapy water, then wipe down with an all-purpose cleaner. If you have one of those detachable shower handles, you could just hose down the shower curtain liner after spraying it with all-purpose cleaner.

If you're in the market for a new shower curtain, I'd recommend a non-PVC liner (see below) and a good organic cotton curtain. This combination will be easiest to clean, since organic cotton naturally repels water and attracts less mildew than cotton that has been treated with pesticides and chemicals. Lifekind (www.lifekind.com) sells a nice shower curtain made of certified organic cotton, and the Gaiam catalog (www.gaiam.com) has one made of pesticide-free, flax-based linen.

Walk-in showers with fiberglass doors are easy to clean, but be careful because these surfaces do scratch, so avoid harsh scouring products. Instead, just wipe them down with an all-purpose cleaner followed by a nontoxic glass cleaner. When you're not using the shower, leave the glass door open to prevent mildew buildup. As always in the bathroom, ventilation is critical.

Spotlight on: PVCs

Most shower-curtain liners are made with polyvinyl chloride, also known as PVC or just vinyl. These days, PVCs are everywhere. Because they're dirt-cheap and easy to manufacture, they're used in a staggering variety of consumer products, from food packaging to children's toys, from piping to automobile parts to umbrellas. When we greened our first hospital, I was shocked to learn that PVCs coated almost every surface—miles and miles of hallway bumpers and railings and all sorts of medical devices. When my environmental center greened Hackensack University Medical Center, it was the first hospital in the country to demand non-PVC bumpers and railings; at the time, the demand just didn't exist.

As consumers, we need to create that demand in other industries as well. While it's extremely difficult to find, for example, a PVC-free shower curtain liner, we still need to take steps to avoid unhealthy products. PVCs in vinyl flooring have been linked to asthma symptoms in children, according to a 1999 study published in the *American Journal of*

Public Health. A study conducted by the National Institute of Public Health in Oslo, Norway, concluded that a child's risk of bronchial obstruction increased with the presence of vinyl flooring in the house. Despite these hazards, the production of PVCs represents the largest and fastest-growing use of chlorine in this country.

PVCs are the absolute worst kind of plastic. Because they're almost impossible to recycle, PVCs create toxic waste products that must be dumped or incinerated. They're made from the flammable gas vinyl chloride, a known human carcinogen. The manufacture and incineration of PVCs can release chlorine-based chemicals, including dioxins, the most harmful man-made substance ever tested.

Toxic Interruption
Phthalates

For the past half century, phthalates—a chemical class that includes dibutyl phthalate, diethyl phthalate, and dimethyl phthalate—have ranked among the most popular plasticizers in the world. These clear, odorless liquids, which resemble common vegetable oil, make vinyl bendable, and artificial scent long-lasting. Phthalates are used in a number of different industries: the manufacture of children's toys, medical devices, nail polish, adhesives, caulk, and paint pigment.

However versatile, phthalates are also known reproductive toxins and environmental pollutants that have been linked to genital mutations in humans and lupus in mice. Exposure to phthalates can lead to infertility, testicular shrinkage, reduced sperm count, and suppressed ovulation. In tests of laboratory animals, phthalates have been shown to disrupt hormones and may cause cancer. Some scientists have speculated that the presence of phthalates in PVCs has contributed to the increased incidences of asthma in this country over the past twenty years, but no long-term research has ever been conducted to confirm or refute this hypothesis.

While all 289 people that the Centers for Disease Control and Prevention tested had some amount of phthalates in their blood, women of childbearing age were found to have the highest levels, probably because manufacturers use phthalates in so many personal-care products, from shampoos to sunscreens. In this country, there are no restrictions on the amount of phthalates companies can use, and this must change.

In 2005, the European Union overcame a powerful industry lobby to place severe restrictions on the use of several different phthalate plasticizers in children's toys and other child-care items. The European Parliament took this controversial stand for one reason alone: to protect children's health. I truly cannot understand why we wouldn't take immediate steps to ban phthalates here as well.

Scouring Tiles

Unless there's a nontoxic scouring product that you really like, I wouldn't recommend buying an abrasive scouring powder just to clean the tiles of your bathtub or shower. You can easily clean those tiles just by rubbing in baking soda with a damp sponge and rinsing, or wiping with vinegar first and following with baking soda or salt as a scouring powder. Because there are no toxins in this formula, it's safe on the grout, too, and you can leave it on for as long as you need. You can go to work, or go pick up your kids at school, without worrying about the tiles getting damaged. You can scour smaller, more stubborn stains using a toothbrush with baking soda, lemon, and salt.

❋   The Toothbrush Trick: While bigger scrub brushes work great on larger surfaces in the bathroom, old toothbrushes are incredibly useful for cleaning in and around the tub. They can get into the cracks and corners of your tub and shower, cleaning between the tiles and in all the small crevices that the larger scrubbers can't reach. A homemade paste of lemon juice and baking soda is usually all you need to enhance the scrubbing power of the toothbrush. When you're finished, soak the toothbrush in vinegar or hydrogen peroxide to prevent bacteria from building up on the bristles.

Soap Scum

To get rid of soap scum in your bathroom, all you need is a good all-purpose cleaner or a nontoxic degreaser and a scrubbing sponge. After giving a surface a good scrub, rinse it off with hot water and the soap scum will be gone.

Cleaning Marble

In recent years, people have begun to use more marble in their bathrooms—marble tubs, marble tiling, and marble flooring have all become popular. Remember, you never want to use vinegar on marble. To clean the marble in my bathroom, I just wipe it down with some hand dishwashing liquid and a little warm water. For tough stains, I sometimes add a little baking soda, but that's pretty much it.

Cleaning Bathroom Fixtures

You can clean most bathroom fixtures—stainless steel, brass or nickel-plated—with a little glass cleaner and a microfiber cloth. Just a quick spray and a wipe is all you'll ever really need most of the time. You can also polish brass with a soft cloth dipped in lemon-and baking-soda solution, or vinegar-and-salt solution. Cleaning silver fixtures is also pretty straightforward: polish every month or so using a special cloth for silver, with or without Weiman Silver Polish.

Cleaning and Deodorizing Toilets

If you're buying a specialty product just to clean your toilet, you may be wasting your money, endangering your family's health, and unnecessarily polluting your water system and the environment. Most of the toilet bowl cleaners and deodorizers being sold at stores right now—like those inserts that turn your water blue every time you flush—are incredibly toxic, polluting you and your water system. They're also completely unnecessary. Here, as in everything, the key is maintenance. With regular up-keep, distilled white vinegar, baking soda, and a little lemon juice will keep your toilet disinfected and odor free.

Spotlight on: Toilet Bowl Cleaners

Toilet bowl cleaners can be acidic and highly toxic, associated with both acute and long-term health effects. Most commercial toilet-bowl cleaners contain a mixture of chlorine bleach and other potentially lethal toxins. These artificially fragranced and colored products contain ingredients that can irritate the skin and worsen already existing respiratory problems.[*]

These products may contain:
- Artificial fragrances
- Chlorine bleach
- Hydrochloric acid
- Naphthalene is a suspected human carcinogen that is especially harmful to small children. An eye and skin irritant, naphthalene can cause cataracts, corneal damage, kidney damage, blood

[*]For detailed information on these toxins, please refer to the Glossary of Chemicals on p. 203.

damage to the fetus, and central nervous system damage. Naphthalene can also promote the breakdown of red blood cells and lead to hemolytic anemia.

- Paradichlorobenzene
- Phosphoric acid
- Sodium bisulfate
- Sodium hydroxide

Suggested Natural Alternatives:

- Remember, routine maintenance is everything. At least once a week, pour a half cup of distilled white vinegar into the back of your toilet bowl, scrub around the whole inside of the toilet, and let it sit for about a half hour before flushing. That's all you'll ever need to do to keep your toilet bowl clean and disinfected.

- To clean the outside of the toilet, spray the toilet seat and the cover with vinegar or a nontoxic all-purpose cleaner and wipe down with a sponge.

- If you have any stains or odor issues and think you need more than a liquid, try using lemon juice and baking soda for the heavy-duty jobs. Combine these three ingredients (vinegar, lemon juice, and baking soda) in the toilet bowl and scrub well. Wait at least half an hour before flushing.

❉ Cleaning Your Scrub Brush: Scrub brushes get nasty fast, so you should replace yours every six months. Be sure to wash it well with hot water, soap, and a little vinegar once a month.

❉ Essential Oil Tip: These blends also work well in the kitchen, or any other room in your house with a high concentration of odors and bacteria. You can use these natural fragrance sprays to spruce up faucets, bathroom fixtures, showerheads, sinks, tiles, woodwork, carpet, and cupboards. In a small (six- or eight-ounce) spray bottle, add two drops of rosemary, four drops of lemon, and three drops of clove. Then fill to the top with distilled water and shake thoroughly. You can also experiment with your own blends of cinnamon, clove, lemongrass, and patchouli. They're all great at disinfecting the air in the bathroom. In my bathroom, I always make patchouli fragrance sprays by putting four to six drops into a six-ounce bottle, then adding the distilled water and shaking it up—people love it. The wonderful scent will linger long after you've left the bathroom.

Bathroom Floors and Mirrors

Carpets and Rugs

As I've already pointed out, you really want to avoid wall-to-wall carpeting in the bathroom. In such a small, naturally damp place, carpeting will encourage the growth of mold and mildew. Instead, you'll want to place just a few small foot rugs or bathmats in front of the sink, toilet, and bathtub. Make sure these are all machine-washable so that you can swap them out regularly, about once a week. I recommend bathmats made out of natural fibers—organic cotton, hemp, jute, and bamboo—which are better at repelling toxins than chemically treated textiles. Organic bamboo mats and towels are also great. I love bamboo—it's naturally antibacterial, and it feels really luxurious and lush, like blended cotton with a little silk woven through it.

Tiled Floors

Again, there's absolutely no reason to buy a specialty product to clean the floors in the bathroom, especially one that contains these toxins:

- Synthetic pine oil
- Petroleum distillates

Suggested Natural Alternative: You can mop your bathroom floors as you mop other floors in your house, with all-purpose cleaner and water, or vinegar and water.

Spotlight on: Glass Cleaners

A Connecticut woman recently wrote me about her curious relationship with glass cleaner: "I could never say why, but I just didn't trust it, especially around my young children. Maybe it was the peculiar smell, or its neon blue color—definitely not a naturally occurring shade! But for whatever reason, I just didn't like using the stuff. When I first saw a non-toxic glass cleaner at the supermarket, I thought why not and threw it in my shopping cart. The first time I used it, I was absolutely thrilled by the results. My windows and mirrors were sparkling and streak-free, and I wasn't repelled by the scent or appearance of the product. I even feel comfortable letting my kids wipe down the glass with me, which I *never* allowed them to do beore."

She was right to suspect that chemical glass and window cleaners and young children don't mix, and good that she did not let her kids near products that might contain ammonia, methanol, and other dangerous toxins.[*]

These products may contain:
- Ammonia
- Butyl cellosolve

[*] For detailed information on these toxins, please refer to the Glossary on p. 203, the Toxic Interruption on ammonia on p. 108, and the Toxic Interruption on butyl cellosolve on p. 156.

- Dioxane—also known as diethylene dioxide, diethylene ether, diethylene oxide—is a carcinogen listed as a hazardous air pollutant in the 1990 Clean Air Act. Dioxane—not the same thing as dioxin—is a solvent classified by the EPA as a probable human carcinogen. It may also suppress the immune system.
- Isopropyl alcohol
- Methanol

"My grandson has terrible asthma, and every time I cleaned the bathroom mirror he would sneeze and his eyes would tear up. On a whim, I bought a nontoxic window cleaner, and I must admit I was amazed. It cleaned the bathroom mirror even better than my old brand, and my grandson wasn't the only one who felt better afterward. For years, my eyes had been tearing up, too, and I hadn't even noticed! I went right back to the store and stocked up on a whole range of nontoxic products—one set for me, and one set for my grandson to take home to his mom! Now, three generations of our family are permanent converts."

Kelly K., Atlanta, GA

Unclogging Drains

Over time, hair and all sorts of other gunk can accumulate in our bathroom drains, and they back up. Prevention is the best cure for this problem—running a cup of vinegar through the drain once a week will minimize the clogging. But if a problem has already developed, I don't recommend using one of the highly corrosive, toxic drain openers you can find in the grocery or hardware store. They can be really rough on your septic system, because they kill the microbial bacteria that are necessary for your septic tank to function properly. Most of the time, these deadly products don't even work and in the end you still wind up calling in a plumber. If you do seek professional assistance, be sure to mention if you've used a commercial drain cleaner so that the necessary protective safety measures can be taken.

Spotlight on: Drain Cleaners

Commercial drain cleaners are among the most corrosive and acutely dangerous of all cleaning products. They work by eating away whatever is clogged in your drain, generating heat to melt down fats into simpler, more easily rinsed substances. But while eating away at your clogs, drain cleaners can also eat away at your skin and pollute your water. The highly corrosive ingredients in drain cleaners can produce dangerous fumes that can get trapped in the enclosed space of your bathroom.*

These products may contain:
- Sodium hydroxide
- Sulfuric acid

Suggested Natural Alternatives: In my experience, toxic products make clogged drains even worse, so after switching to nontoxic cleaning agents, in time, your drain problem might resolve itself. Until then, try the following tips.

- First, try plunging or using a pressurized drain opener, but not after using any commercial drain opener. If the drain-opening liquid splashes back in your face, it could blind you.

- If that doesn't work, pour boiling water, a half-cup of vinegar, and four tablespoons of baking soda down the clogged drain. Cover the drain

---

*For detailed information on these toxins, refer to the Glossary of Chemicals on p. 203.

for half an hour, then rinse. But do not use this method after trying a commercial drain opener—the vinegar can react with the drain opener to create dangerous fumes.

• If you pour this mixture of vinegar, a little baking soda for deodorizing, and some boiling water down your drain once a week, you should be clog-free for life.

• You can also try pouring some natural enzyme cleaner down your drain to prevent future buildup.

"The drain in our downstairs bathroom was so clogged up that I got in the habit of buying a big bottle of drain opener every time I went to the grocery store. I was so frightened that one of our kids would find their way into the bathroom that I even bought a big DO NOT ENTER sign to hang on the door after treating the drain. The bathroom stank for hours afterward, but what could I do? Calling in a plumber seemed too expensive for such a 'minor' problem. But then my husband pointed out that I was spending about $10 a week on these drain cleaners, so eventually we decided to seek professional help. After the plumber cleaned out our drain, he recommended we pour white vinegar down it on a weekly basis to keep the drain open. I couldn't believe how well this trick worked—we never had a clogged drain again! I was no longer wasting money on terrible-smelling drain cleaners, and I no longer had any use for that DO NOT ENTER sign!"

Meredith M., Westhampton, NY

Toxic Interruption

Formaldehyde

Though we've known for two decades that formaldehyde causes cancer in humans, we're still using this hazardous preservative in a wide range of household cleaning products, including deodorizers, disinfectants, and germicides. This must change. For our own safety, we need to get rid of all formaldehyde-coated items in our homes: mattresses, permanent-press fabrics, "wrinkle-resistant" sheets, cabinets, wallpapers, floor and furniture finishes . . . We're exposed to formaldehyde all day, every day, and we don't even know it.

Formaldehyde belongs to a class of chemicals known as volatile organic compounds, or VOCs, which become gases at room temperature. Airborne formaldehyde—a major contributor to indoor air pollution—is a strong respiratory irritant that can make the eyes, nose, and throat tingle. Even at very low levels of exposure, formaldehyde can have toxic effects. It can make the chest constrict and tighten, and cause insomnia, dizziness, nausea, nosebleeds, skin rashes, and headaches. In the 1970s and early '80s, scientists studied the health effects of urea formaldehyde foam insulation. After learning how dangerous it was, in 1982 the U.S. Consumer Product Safety Commission outlawed the installation of formaldehyde foam insulation in new construction. Later, the U.S. Department of Housing and Urban Development set strict limits on the amount of formaldehyde that can be used in residential construction. But even after the EPA listed it as a probable human carcinogen in 1987, companies are still using formaldehyde in many consumer items.

Chapter 7

The Bedroom

Your Sanctuary

Your bedroom should be a sanctuary: clean, simple, and peaceful, a place conducive to rest and relaxation. Sleep, as we all know, is a hugely important component of a healthy life. It controls your metabolism, your mood, and your overall sense of well-being. Your bedroom can either encourage, or disturb, this process. And so, though it's not always practical, particularly in urban areas and smaller spaces, you should make every effort to minimize clutter in your bedroom. Keep the decor simple and your possessions to a minimum. It's much healthier not to have a TV, or any other extraneous electrical gadget, in your bedroom. VCRs and computers and phones and clock radios and all those other items we typically keep near our beds emit a lot of electromagnetic energy that can reduce the quality of our sleep. These distractions don't belong in the place where you're supposed to be relaxing and escaping the commotion of your busy lives.

It makes common sense to arrange your bedroom in a way that promotes healthy sleep. If you truly want to green your home, you need to do more than just buy nontoxic products: you need make every aspect of your life healthier, too. Remember—your physical environment should heal, not harm, you. Try to keep this objective in mind as you read through this chapter.

Vacuuming and Dusting

Vacuuming

Vacuuming is an essential part of housecleaning, especially if anyone in your family suffers from allergies or asthma. In general, we rely too heavily on products to clean our homes instead of just dry mopping or vacuuming on a regular basis. To keep the levels of dust and particulate toxins low in your home, I recommend vacuuming at least once or twice a week. I regularly pour baking soda on my carpets and rugs and vacuum it up to deodorize the fabrics.

But be careful, because some vacuum cleaners—particularly the bagless models—have a tendency to rerelease dust or other particles back into the atmosphere, which can really irritate sensitive members of your household.

You should also look into the HEPA vacuums for asthma sufferers. These can be expensive, though, and a recent *Consumer Reports* survey concluded that the overall design of the vacuum cleaner is often more important than any special filtration features.

Different types of vacuum cleaners serve different needs:

• Upright vacuums are generally the cheapest, and they're great for cleaning carpets.

• Canister vacuums are recommended for cleaning drapes, upholstery, and under furniture. They're easy to store and great for small spaces.

• Cordless vacuums are convenient for light to moderate cleaning jobs. If you live in a small apartment, they also take up very little room.

- **Stick and hand vacuums** lack the power of larger models and work best for small jobs and quick cleanups.

The *Consumer Reports* survey also evaluated the most efficient and best-value vacuum cleaners available right now. It found that models with a manual pile-height adjustment are useful for cleaning carpets, and that a brush on/off switch will help avoid scattering dust when cleaning bare floors.

But whichever model you pick, before using your new vacuum cleaner for the first time, be sure to read the instructions thoroughly. So many people break vacuums because they never bother learning how to use them properly. You should change the vacuum bags or empty the canister on a regular basis to prolong the life of your vacuum cleaner.

✳ **Essential Oil Tip:** If you have a bag vacuum, try saturating a disposable cloth or tissue and placing it in the collecting bag. As you clean, the oil will diffuse around the room. If your vacuum collects dirt into a water reservoir, add a few drops before cleaning for the same effect.

Dusting

Dusting is essential for those hard-to-reach places beyond the orbit of your vacuum cleaner. The dust in your house is a mixture of particles from activities as varied as cooking, cleaning, and smoking. It may also contain pollutants brought in from outdoors, including pollen, pesticides, heavy metals, and dander from pets' fur. You should dust regularly—several times a week—to prevent these toxins from accumulating, as they have a tendency to do indoors.

For dusting in high places, use a long-handled tool, lint-free or microfiber cloth, and nontoxic glass cleaner. Mist the cloth with glass cleaner and dust all surfaces—the tops of doors, fans, vents, and cabinets—above eye level to ensure that the dust will not fly everywhere in the air. High-dust regularly to prevent dust from accumulating in places above eye level. Clean dust mop or microfiber cloth when soiled.

Closets

Closet Organization

People have all sorts of different bedroom closets in their homes: walk-in closets, traditional closets with one or two hanging rods, coat closets, armoire cabinets, portable storage wardrobes. No matter what size or shape the closet, it's important that you keep it organized. Every season—or at the very least once a year, in early spring—spend a few hours reassessing what's in your clothes closet.

I have a rule: for every new piece of clothing I bring into my closet, I give away one (or more) old piece. We usually end up wearing the same things over and over anyway, so it's important to be realistic about which clothes to keep.

In the winter, when we keep our windows closed more often, our clothes don't get as aired out as they should. Spring cleaning is a great time to take inventory of everything that's been stashed away. Remove all the clothes that you won't be wearing for the next few months—they're just taking up space and collecting dust. If your closet is on the small side, consider storing out-of-season clothes in airtight containers in another part of the house. Your goal should be to pare down the contents of your closet to the absolute essentials.

If you clean and organize your closet regularly, you'll always know where everything is, which will make dressing a lot easier in the morning. With maintenance, you can also avoid the accumulation of dust, insects, and other creatures that like to hide in the crevices of dark closets. You should never store clothes on the floor of your closet, only shoes—and it's best to keep floors completely clear. If you store your shoes off the ground, you'll cut down on dust and make it easier to vacuum in there. Consider getting raked shelving for your shoes or one of those hanging devices to keep your shoes off the floor.

A Note on Shoes

Here's an easy way to cut down on your cleaning: Leave your shoes at the front door. When you're walking down the street, especially in urban and suburban areas, your shoes come into contact with tons of different pollutants: germs, dirt, bacteria, pesticides, fungicides, even animal feces. Do you really want to track all of this gunk into your home?

In my house, we have a rule: Whoever you are, your shoes come off at the front door and you leave them there. Shoes worn outdoors do not travel around the house—it just makes no common sense. When we're at home, we walk around barefoot, or in our socks, or in a special pair of slippers or sneakers reserved for indoor use only.

In addition to guests, every once in a while, most of us have workers or repairmen enter our house—a cable guy, or a meter reader, or someone to fix the refrigerator or telephone line. Recently, my sister called me really upset because a painter had clomped through her living room with muddy shoes. I told her that she should have asked the man to remove his shoes or—if that wasn't practical—asked him to cover them with blue booties before entering her house. I buy these booties by the box and keep them in a closet by the door for this purpose, though most of the time this isn't even necessary. I told my sister that when she next calls to make an appointment, she can simply request that the painter brings booties with him. It's the policy of most service companies to keep supplies of these booties, but for whatever reason, most workers choose not to wear them.

Dry Cleaning in Closets

Avoid taking your clothes to a toxic dry cleaner. PERC (perchlorethylene) and other man-made organic solvents used by traditional dry cleaners are highly bioaccumulative toxins that have been found in breast tissue and even breast milk. PERC, which can do long-term damage to the liver, kidneys, and eyesight, is responsible for 90 percent of all groundwater pollution in this country. That's right—90 percent! But though the EPA listed PERC as a hazardous air pollutant almost a decade ago, roughly 80 percent of professional dry cleaners are still using this lethal chemical to clean their customers' clothes.

Dry-cleaning technology is improving rapidly, however, and as the consumer demand grows, we're seeing more and more alternatives to PERC. Over the past ten years, three new processes have been developed to clean clothes without dangerous chemicals, for roughly the same price as the traditional toxic cleaners. Just go to the computer and Google the dry cleaners in your neighborhood to find out the options available to you. If you can't find a nontoxic alternative, put the pressure on your local dry cleaner to make the switch to green cleaning processes—I promise this community petitioning works. In New York, dry cleaners stopped using PERC for one reason and one reason alone: because their customers demanded it.

Most popular nontoxic dry-cleaning options:

1. Carbon dioxide cleaning: A liquid carbon dioxide solvent replaces PERC with equal efficacy. Carbon dioxide cleaning is also great for delicate clothes.

2. Silicone-based cleaning solvent: The company GreenEarth has developed a cleaning process using siloxane, a solvent that cleans without harmful chemicals. For more information on liquid silicone dry cleaning, visit www.greenearthcleaning.com.

3. Wet dry cleaning: "Wet" dry cleaning employs industrial-size machines that operate similarly to washing machines. But despite the use of soap and water, wet dry-cleaning machines are much gentler on your clothes, with special equipment designed to prevent shrinkage and maintain the shape of your garments.

Even if you're switched over to a nontoxic cleaner, you should still always take the plastic wrap off before putting the clothes into your closet. If possible, get rid of it before it even enters your house. The plastic traps the chemicals on your clothes so that it all just cooks inside your closet.

If you want to be even more green, you should consider buying a few cloth garment bags from Linens 'n Things or Bed Bath & Beyond or any other home store. They sell beautiful garment bags now—some even in organic cotton—that you can reuse again and again. Write your name on the bag with a Sharpie or some other nontoxic permanent marker, and when you drop off your clothes at the dry cleaner, ask them to hang the clean clothes in your garment bag. Most dry cleaners are happy to provide this small service, especially since you'll be saving them the cost of the plastic wrap.

Spotlight on: Mothballs and Moth Crystals

Last summer, the same afternoon that a new batch of kids showed up at the ranch, I started smelling mothballs from the other end of a long hallway in the hacienda where we all live together. I've obviously never used mothballs—they contain incredibly toxic carcinogens that can damage the liver, kidneys, blood, eyes, and nervous system. They leave an unpleasantly persistent odor on your clothes and can be lethal when inhaled.

Storing mothballs in small, unventilated places like closets and drawers only compounds their toxic effects. You should never, ever have these dangerous pesticides in a house with children, who have been known to mistake the gray, solid balls for candy. Children have even been poisoned just by wearing clothing that has been treated with mothballs, which suggests that the toxins in mothballs can be easily absorbed through the skin. Chemically sensitive individuals are also particularly at risk.

Knowing all of these hazards, I gathered all the kids together and asked them if any of them had brought mothballs in their luggage, or if maybe their mothers stored their clothes in mothballs at home. Now, I was bowled over when not one but two of the kids raised their hands and admitted that they'd brought along these little screw-top glass vials filled with loose crystals of mothballs. I couldn't believe it—we're talking about kids with cancer here, remember. They explained that they take a little pinch out of the vial and sprinkle mothballs around their bed, on the backboard, and all over the floor. Mothballs, they told me, help them sleep and ward off evil spirits.

After educating the kids about mothballs, I immediately got to work removing all traces of them. To get rid of the toxins in the air, I turned on the fan and opened the windows and doors for cross-ventilation. I vacuumed the bed area, mattress, and floor around it. (When I was done, I had to throw out the vacuum bag, which the mothballs had completely contaminated.) After vacuuming, I mopped the floor with my all-purpose cleaner diluted in water. Finally, I diffused essential oils in the boys' rooms for an hour. You can use a number of essential oils for this purpose. I prefer Dr. Young's Thieves blend, a mixture of lemon, clove, cinnamon, and rosemary that has been proven to disinfect the air.

To save yourself these hassles, don't use mothballs in the first place. They can have an extremely negative impact on our health, with ingredients that might cause central nervous system damage or even cancer.*

*For detailed information on these toxins, please refer to the Glossary of Chemicals on p. 203.

These products may contain:
- Naphthalene
- Paradichlorobenzene

Suggested Natural Alternatives: You can experiment with many different safe and easy methods to keep your clothes moth free.

- If feasible, consider building a cedar closet where you can store your clothes. Or place cedar balls and blocks of cedar wood in your drawers, and between sweaters and winter coats. Sand the cedar regularly to refresh. And remember, whenever you use cedar, you need to make sure that the wood has not been treated with any pesticides or chemicals.

- Vacuum rugs, carpets, and upholstered furniture regularly.

- Store seasonal woolens in airtight containers when not in use. Every year when spring cleaning comes around, put away the clothes you won't be wearing until the next winter.

- Clean woollens prior to storage. They should be hand-washed using a mild nontoxic laundry liquid whenever necessary. Dry clean as last resort.

- As often as you can, air your clothes in direct sunlight.

- A number of essential oils work just as well as mothballs: citronella, lavender, lemongrass, Western red cedar, or rosemary, depending on which scent you prefer. To make a sachet, saturate a cotton ball with one of these oils and then tie this inside a small handkerchief or cotton square. Then hang these cloths where you keep your clothes. Cedar chips and bay leaves are also good for repelling moths. Refresh the sachets as often as you find necessary.

- Washing your clothes with an essential oil–based product like Eucalan (www.eucalan.com) will help keep the moths away.

- Kill moth eggs by running garments through a warm clothes dryer.

- Periodically shake out woollens. Discard or donate woollens, leathers, and feather products that are no longer used to avoid contaminating newer materials.

- If you suspect an infestation, place the item in a plastic bag in the freezer for at least forty-eight hours. Return the item to room temperature and repeat freezing. Leave item in a tightly sealed plastic bag or container to prevent reinfestation.

※ Essential Oil Tip: Put sachets of essential oil blends—I love rose and patchouli—in your drawers where you would ordinarily place the mothballs to impart a clean, fresh scent to your clothes. For children's sleepwear, Roman chamomile is pleasant and relaxing.

Natural Mothballs

Follow this recipe to make all-natural sachets to keep all your clothes smelling clean and fresh without toxins. You can buy most of these herbs dried and in bulk at your local health food store:

- 2 ounces of dried rosemary
- 2 ounces of mint

- 1 ounce of dried thyme
- 1 ounce of ginseng
- 8 ounces of whole cloves

Combine the ingredients in a large bowl and blend. Make sachets by choosing a four-inch-square piece of natural fiber with a tight weave, such as silk. Sew three sides together, then fill with the herbs and sew the fourth side shut. You can adapt this pattern to any size you want (a two-inch square is the traditional size for the undergarments drawer). For small sachets, you can fill empty cotton teabags, which are sold at most health-food stores. If you're in a rush, just tie the herbs up in a cotton bandana or handkerchief. Place the herbs in the middle, gather the edges together, and tie with a ribbon.

Other alternatives worth trying:
- Cedar blocks (sand regularly to refresh)
- Cedar shavings (pet rodent bedding)
- Bay leaves
- Cinnamon sticks
- Cloves
- Lemon
- Sweet woodruff
- Tansy
- Eucalyptus
- Lavender
- Mint
- Peppercorns
- Rosemary
- Vetiver
- Wormwood

Cleaning and Deodorizing Carpets

Soiled carpets and rugs detract from interior spaces and create the wrong impression for visitors. Incorrectly treating these fabrics can actually set a stain rather than remove or minimize it. As I've said many times already, the less carpeting you have, the easier it will be to keep your home clean and healthy. But carpeting and rug manufacturing remains an $8.5 billion-a-year industry in this country, so chances are you do have some carpeting in your house. If so, you need to make sure you're cleaning it properly. Most traditional carpet-cleaning products are both toxic and ineffective at getting stains out.

> "My living-room carpet is off-white and almost impossible to clean, so whenever I entertained at home, I was careful never to serve red wine. But one night, some friends of ours brought over a bottle of Merlot, and I felt rude not uncorking it right away. Of course, within ten minutes, my worst nightmare came true—my friend's husband splashed almost half a glass of wine all over the carpet. I tried to act calm and pretend I didn't care, but I was panicking inside, thinking about the cost of getting the whole room recarpeted. Since I'd previously used chemical cleaners on the smaller carpet stains with disappointing results—the affected area would turn an unattractive yellow-brown—I decided to spray a nontoxic cleaner on the wine stains. To my complete and total amazement, the product lifted the wine right off, and unlike the cleaners I'd used before, it left no traces. My carpet was as good as new and in under a minute I was able to devote my full attention to my guests!"
>
> Ellie S., Washington, DC

Spotlight on: Carpet Cleaners and Deodorizers

Most specialty rug shampoos are designed to dissolve greasy stains in the fabric, holding them in suspension until you can remove them. Some products also coat surfaces to repel soil in advance. To clean your carpets, you should never resort to these traditional carpet cleaners, which are filled with harsh chemicals and artificial fragrances that can be irritating and harmful to people, especially children and those with allergies.*

These products may contain:
- Aerosol propellants
- Artificial fragrances
- Naphthalene
- Perchlorethylene (PERC)
- Triethanolamine (TEA) is a group of synthetic surfactants that can irritate the eyes, skin, and respiratory tract. With prolonged exposure, TEA can cause permanent skin sensitization.

Suggested Natural Alternatives: A number of green companies make nontoxic carpet cleaners that often cost less than the standard brands. Some nontoxic all-purpose cleaners are also great at cleaning carpets. Keeping your carpet clean the natural way is better for people and extends the life of your carpet. And remember, spot cleaning between general shampooing can save time and cut the cost of carpet shampoo. Here's how to use these products:

1. Spray directly on the soiled area.
2. Agitate the spot with a small brush from the outside of the spot

* For detailed information on these toxins, please refer to the Glossary of Chemicals on p. 203.

inward. (A toothbrush works well for small stains, or use a small scrub brush for larger stains.)

3. With a white cloth, blot the spot gently. Do not rub; instead, press the rag down on the spot until soil disappears. Repeat if necessary.

4. For tough stains, add hot water to the spot after brushing, and blot as above.

Bedding and Linens

Healthy sleep depends on a healthy physical environment. When you rest, you should be breathing clean air, not air contaminated with PERC, pesticides, volatile organic compounds, and formaldehyde. Because we spend so many hours with bedding close to our skin, we should pay close attention to what type of linens we choose to buy and how we clean them. Even if you use nontoxic laundry products, if you're sleeping on sheets coated with pesticides, you're fooling yourself. I don't care if you bought your sheets at Pratesi or Kmart; if they're cotton, they're probably packed with chemicals. The textile industry uses pesticides at just about every stage of the manufacturing process.

Cotton is the most heavily sprayed crop in this country, and that's saying something. Every year, cotton growers use nearly 10 percent of the world's pesticides and almost a quarter of the world's insecticides. Even worse: Many of the pesticides sprayed on cotton crops are organophospates, which were first developed as toxic nerve agents during World War II. In spraying our cotton crops with pesticides, we're ruining our fields and exposing our workers—and everyone else in the community—to toxins, which become airbone while they're being sprayed. Do you really want to place your skin next to these chemicals for eight hours every night?

When shopping for cotton sheets, you should know that they fall into three categories. The healthiest sheets you can buy are labeled "or-

ganic cotton," meaning the cotton is pure—grown *and* processed without pesticides. The next-best choice is "green cotton," meaning chemicals are used during the farming but not the manufacturing process. In
the third category are "regular" cotton sheets, or ones made from cotton
that has been treated with chemicals during both the growing and manufacturing stages. Of these, you most of all want to avoid sheets labeled
"easy care" or "no iron." These sheets—generally the cheapest in most
stores—have probably been treated with formaldehyde resins.

Ideally, instead of buying sheets packed with pesticides and
formaldehyde resins, you should consider investing over time in ecofriendly bedding. Organic linens are so much healthier than traditional
treated cotton, and you don't have to sacrifice aesthetic value or pay too
much money to get them.

You can find a great selection of organic cotton and bamboo linens
from the Gaiam catalog (www.gaiam.com), which often has great sales
on their Web site. Coyuchi (www.coyuchiorganic.com) also makes great
organic cotton sheets. Whole Foods now sells a line of organic linens and
pillows. ABC Carpet and Home in New York also has a great selection of
linens and mattresses.

The same principles apply to mattresses, which commonly contain
pesticides, fungicides, fumigants, formaldehyde, flame retardants, and
other toxins. A wool mattress is by far the safest alternative. Naturally
bacteria and mildew resistant, wool also keeps you warm in the winter
and cool in the summer, since its fibers can absorb 30 percent of their
weight in body vapors. With a little bargain-hunting on Froogle.com or
eBay, you can probably find these mattresses for about the same price as
the toxic standard models. A great selection of organic wool mattress
pads is also available. I always recommend getting one of those zip-on
mattress covers to reduce potential allergens in the bedroom. You can
find these just about anywhere.

It's good to replace your mattress every eight to ten years—if for no other reason than that old mattresses often don't give adequate support to your back. *Dwell* magazine recently did a story on the great selection of organic, healthy mattresses now being made. You should know that these mattresses aren't available everywhere, or affordable to everyone.

• The Swedish company Hästens (www.hastens.com) makes great all-natural mattresses and other bedroom accessories. They're handmade of horsehair, flax, wool soaked in fire-retardant sea salt, and cotton.

• Royal Pedic (www.royal-pedic.com) makes petrochemical-free latex perforated with lamb's wool and organic cotton.

• Magniflex Duoform (www.magniflex.com) sells water-based polyurethane foam and visco-elastic "memory" foam that's made from the natural fibers of aloe, green tea, merino wool, corn, silk, cashmere, and bamboo.

• Green Sleep (www.greensleep.com) makes beds from chemical-free rubber sap, hand-picked cotton, organic silk, and wool with lanolin, which naturally repels dust mites.

Toxic Interruption
Phenols

Phenol—also known as alkyl phenoxy polyethoxy ethanol or nonyl phenoxy ethoxylate—is a known mutagen and suspected carcinogen found on at least eight different federal regulatory lists. It's a skin irritant, too, which can cause swelling and burn skin, eyes, nose, mouth, throat, and lungs. Oral exposure to large amounts of phenol has been linked to anorexia, reduced fetal body weight, abnormal development, and growth retardation.

Phenol can also interfere with the ability of the blood to carry oxygen and cause bronchitis to develop. Higher exposures can cause a buildup of fluid in the lungs, which can lead to pulmonary edema. Internal consumption can lead to circulatory collapse, convulsions, cold sweats, coma, and death.

Despite these perils, phenols are used in many different consumer products: throat lozenges, ointments, ear and nose drops, and mouthwashes. Household cleaners that may contain phenols include disinfectants and all-purpose cleaners, furniture polishes and waxes, metal polishes and cleaners, and laundry detergents.

Chapter 8

Living Areas

Home Sweet Home: Deodorizing Naturally

Most commercial air-freshening products, in whatever form they take—candles, potpourri, or plug-ins—are incredibly toxic. When I was a kid, I saw a lot of jelly-filled discs in friends' bathrooms. They'd sit on the countertop until the jelly dried up, and then would promptly be replaced.

I really want to encourage everyone to move away from these highly toxic products. When we're exposed to these chemicals on a daily basis, they accumulate in our blood and contribute to a number of serious health problems. The more we eliminate these toxins from our environment, the healthier we'll be.

Spotlight on: Air Fresheners and Deodorizers

Solid air fresheners may contain pollutants that can damage the lungs if inhaled in high concentration for prolonged periods of time. If accidentally ingested by children or pets, they can be poisonous and even fatal. Most formulas are flammable and are derived from petroleum by-products.*

*For more information on these toxins, please refer to the Glossary of Chemicals on p. 203, as well as the petroleum distillates Toxic Interruption on p. 58 and the formaldehyde Toxic Interruption on p. 127.

These products may contain:
- Aerosol propellants
- Artificial fragrances
- Formaldehyde
- Methylene chloride
- Naphthalene
- Paradichlorobenzene—also known as p-dichlorobenzene, PDCB, 1,4-dichlorobenzene—is an extremely toxic, volatile carcinogen and endocrine disrupter that causes liver and kidney damage. Its vapors can irritate the skin, eyes, and respiratory tract. Paradichlorobenzene does not biodegrade.
- Petroleum distillates
- Synthetic pine oil

Suggested Natural Alternatives: Even many air-freshening products that advertise "French lavender" or "natural apricot" in their formulas may also contain artificial fragrances and other dangerous chemicals. Sometimes, in fact, these "natural" additives function merely as scents that mask the chemicals present in a product. And in the vast majority of cases, the additives are themselves chemical.

To deodorize your home, I recommend the commonsense approach: air it out, open windows even in winter, put baking soda on the rugs, and eliminate all toxins wherever possible. Use essential oils: they are far more concentrated and last much longer than artificial fragrances—and they also smell a lot nicer. Essential oils have been produced for almost a thousand years by now. They've long been renowned for their sterilizing properties: the Egyptians treated as many as eighty-one different diseases with aromatic herbs like myrrh oil and honey. During the fifteenth-century plague in Europe, when people all over the continent were dropping dead of infectious disease, four French thieves became notorious for robbing the recently departed without becoming infected themselves. When at last they were captured, they revealed the secret of their trade: a concoction of cloves, rosemary, cinnamon, eucalyptus radiata, and lemon that they rubbed on their hands, ears, and temples.

In other words, essential oils don't just smell great; they have significant health benefits. When diffused inside your home, they actually increase the amount of oxygen in the atmosphere. Oils like frankincense help you breathe better, transporting oxygen and other nutrients into your cells and into your brain. When diffused in the entryway of a house, they can destroy pet odors, attack mildew, and absorb airborne dust particles. Essential oils are by far the healthiest, cleanest way to deodorize your home.

"At the age of 42, I was hospitalized with bronchitis. Though I'd never had any history of respiratory problems before, I left the hospital with asthma and a ton of new allergies. When I got back home, nothing was the same. The perfume I'd worn for years and years now made me sneeze uncontrollably and reach for my inhaler. The spray air freshener I loved so much produced the same reaction—utter misery. I immediately got rid of all these asthma triggers, but not without considerable regret. For the next five years, I used only unscented, hypoallergenic products. Dull, dull, dull. And then one day I learned about essential oils from a massage therapist I met at the hairdresser. I can honestly say that this discovery changed my life. I now diffuse essential oils in every room of my home and blend them together to make really wonderful perfumes—and my lungs never object. Just because I have asthma and allergies, I don't have to live in a completely scent-free world."

Cassie S., Pottersville, NJ

There are lots of ways you can incorporate essential oils into your life:

- Purchase a diffuser. I prefer cold diffusers, since burning can compromise the constitution of the oil. You can buy cold diffusers at www.youngliving.com and www.abundanthealth4u.com.

- Add essential oils to cedar chips to make your own potpourri.

- Deodorize drawers and closets with sachets of scented cedar chips.

- Put any conifer essential oil—spruce, fir, cedar, or pine—onto each log in your fireplace. As the logs burn, a wonderful evergreen scent will fill the room.

- Douse cotton balls in your favorite essential oil and place them in the air vents of your home or car.

- Place a bowl of water and a few drops of your favorite oil on a wood stove.

- Place a damp cloth with a few drops of essential oil on it near the intake duct of your heating and cooling system.

To get you started with experimenting, here are a few brief descriptions of some of the most popular essential oils available in most health food stores. If you get hooked and want to learn more, consider buying a book on the subject on www.abundanthealth4u.com.

- Citrus: soothing, reduces tension and depression
- Frankincense: increases mental activity
- Lavender: helps you sleep; relieves stress, depression, and tension

- **Lemongrass:** calms the nerves; soothes headaches
- **Peppermint:** clears nasal passages; repels bugs
- **Rosemary:** enhances memory; invigorating
- **Pine:** respiratory antiseptic, reduces anxiety and stress levels
- **Sage:** cleansing and detoxifying; relieves mental strain and exhaustion

My favorite book on essential oils, *Essential Oils Desk Reference,* provides this classic recipe for freshening the air:

- Ten drops lemon
- Six drops bergamot
- Five drops lime
- Five drops grapefruit

Dilute the blended oils with distilled water in spray bottle, shake well, and squirt as needed.

Polishing Up

Spotlight on: Furniture Polishes and Waxes

The specialty wood-cleaning products that we use to polish our wood floors, tables, and other pieces of furniture can be flammable, toxic, and highly irritating. Their ingredients might include known human carcinogens and mutagens.*

---

*For detailed information on these toxins, please refer to the Glossary of Chemicals on p. 203, as well as the ammonia Toxic Interruption on p. 108, the phenols Toxic Interruption on p. 144, and the petroleum distillates Toxic Interruption on p. 58.

These products may contain:
- Aerosol propellants
- Ammonia
- Benzene
- Morpholine is an extremely toxic chemical that irritates the skin, eyes, and mucous membranes. Reacts with nitrites to form carcinogenic nitrosamines, and may cause liver and kidney damage.
- Phenol
- Petroleum distillates
- Trichlorethane (TCA)
- Toluene

Suggested Natural Alternatives:

- I would lay off the products altogether when it comes to cleaning and polishing antique wooden pieces. Most of the time, it's safest just to dust these items with a microfiber cloth. At the ranch, we have a bunch of wooden antiques—armoires and bookshelves and chests and desks—that we never polish. If you want to safeguard your antique wood from bleaching, just be sure to keep it out of the sun.

- To clean and polish wooden furniture and floors with a high-gloss finish or to moisturize matte wood, I use essential oil of lemon with organic olive oil. For a floor, take a cup of olive oil and add seven drops of lemon, then dry mop. For a table, use a tablespoon of olive oil and a couple of drops of lemon esssential oil on a cloth. Then just rub it into the table until it's absorbed. You only need to do this about once a year for great results. Safe alternatives are available from environmentally responsible companies. Ecover has a wood floor polish with linseed oil, and Williamsville Wax makes a great product, too.

• For waxing wooden furniture or flooring with a high-gloss finish, avoid products that contain paraffin, mineral oil, or other petroleum distillates. Opt for less toxic alternatives with linseed oil or beeswax as the base ingredients. For a great shine, you can also just buff the furniture by hand with beeswax and a microfiber cloth or a chamois.

Spotlight on: Metal Polishes and Cleaners

Metal cleaners, which are designed to remove stains and polish metal, are for the most part abrasive, flammable, and highly toxic. Their ingredients might include suspected carcinogens, respiratory and gastrointestinal irritants, and neurotoxins and nervous system depressants. Other ingredients, like hydrofluoric acid and phosphoric acid, are major air pollutants.*

These products may contain:
- Aerosol propellants
- Ammonia
- Crystalline silica
- Hydrofluoric acid
- Organic solvents
- Oxalic acid
- Petroleum distillates
- Phenol
- Phosphoric acid is an eye, skin, and respiratory irritant featured on the EPA's Community Right-to-Know list and controlled as

---

*For detailed information on these toxins, please refer to the Glossary of Chemicals on p. 203, as well as the ammonia Toxic Interruption on p. 108, the petroleum distillates Toxic Interruption on p. 58, and the phenols Toxic Interruption on p. 144.

an air pollutant under the Clean Air Act. If inhaled, phosphoric
acid vapors can make lungs burn.
- Sulfuric acid
- Thioureas

Suggested Natural Alternatives: Every metal has unique properties, so
it doesn't make sense to use the same methods to clean and polish different types. Rather than purchasing expensive metal-cleaning products,
why not rely on your usual household staples?

- Aluminum: Clean aluminum with a solution of cream of tartar
and water.

- Brass: Polish brass with a soft cloth dipped in a lemon-and-
baking-soda solution, or a vinegar-and-salt solution.

- Chrome: Polish chrome with a nontoxic glass cleaner and a microfiber cloth.

- Copper: Clean tarnished copper using a cloth, soft sponge, or
rag, and a mixture of salt, lemon juice, and water. Be sure to dry the copper thoroughly after washing.

- Gold: Clean gold with toothpaste.

- Pewter: Pewter can be cleaned with a paste of salt, vinegar, and
flour.

- Stainless steel: Clean stainless steel with nontoxic glass cleaner
and a microfiber cloth. To get rid of water damage on utensils, soak them
in baking soda for fifteen minutes, then rinse and wipe dry. I soak my
stainless steel flatware once a year.

- Silver: With silver, maintenance is key. Storing your silver in cloths will reduce your dependence on toxic silver polishes. Sometimes I find it necessary to use Weiman Silver Polish, which seems to be the most benign product for heavy-duty silver polishing. But because even Weiman's contains petroleum distillates, I use it sparingly and not very often at all. For smaller jobs, you can just use a little soap and warm water, or a silver-polishing cloth. You can also polish silver by making a paste out of one part water and three parts baking soda. Apply this paste to your silver with a cloth, rinse with cool water, and polish to a shine. (You can use toothpaste the same way, as long as it's a paste and not a gel.)

Cleaning Crystal

You don't need to buy any fancy specialty products to clean crystal. Just use a soft cloth—not a paper towel, but a fresh microfiber cloth or chamois—and wipe the crystal down by hand. That's all you'll ever need to do. For added polish, put a little glass cleaner on the cloth. You can also polish crystal glasses and tableware with the certified organic cotton kitchen towels sold in the Lifekind catalog (www.lifekind.com).

Cleaning Drapes and Upholstery

Cleaning drapes and upholstery isn't as challenging as some of us might think. Here, again, regular maintenance is the key. Vacuuming your drapes and upholstery works much better than specialty upholstery cleaners, which contain flammable toxins that irritate the eyes and skin, and even cause serious birth defects. I recommend taking drapes to a green dry cleaner once a year for regular maintenance. If your drapes get stained by water or any other substance, take them to a nontoxic dry cleaner as soon as possible.

Spotlight on: Upholstery Cleaners

Toxic upholstery cleaners do little more than take up precious storage space in your home. They contain ingredients that may be harmful to your family and the environment.* I never use them.

These products may contain:
- Aerosol propellants
- Butyl cellosolve

Toxic Interruption
Butyl Cellosolve

Also known as 2-butoxyethanol, butyl oxitol, ethylene glycol monobutyl ether, butyl cellosolve is a neurotoxin that can depress the nervous system. This synthetic solvent and grease cutter, an ingredient in many different cleaning products, can irritate mucous membranes and cause liver and kidney damage. In the short term, butyl cellosolve can irritate the eyes, nose, throat, and mouth, in addition to causing headaches, dizziness, lightheadedness, confusion, and even loss of consciousness. But the chronic health effects are even scarier. Butyl cellosolve, a suspected teratogen, can damage both developing fetuses and male reproductive glands. It is also suspected of contributing to learning disabilities among children. Look out for products containing butyl cellosolve, for some companies claiming to be "green" still use this toxin in their formulas.

*For detailed information on these toxins, please refer to the Glossary of Chemicals on p. 203, as well as the butyl cellosolve Toxic Interruption on this page.

Suggested Natural Alternatives:

- To maintain drapes and upholstery, especially the heavier fabrics, in good condition, be sure to vacuum them regularly. You don't need to scrub them down all the time. For major sprucing up, I take my draperies every year to a nontoxic dry cleaner.

- You can also use a nontoxic laundry liquid to clean delicate fabrics, curtains, upholstery, and even antique rugs. All-purpose cleaner can also work great on carpets and floors—much better than any expensive specialty spot-removing product.

- If you live in a region with high levels of mold and mildew, I recommend experimenting with Dr. Young's Melrose blend, which is known for its antifungal and antimold properties. Dilute the Melrose in a spray bottle with distilled water and mist your draperies weekly.

Pest Control

It doesn't make much sense to clean your home with natural products if you're going to call in a professional exterminator twice a year. The chemicals used by professional exterminating services are toxic beyond belief. All over the country, people hire firms to set off roach bombs and flea bombs in their houses and apartments. After they leave the house and send their kids off to school, the exterminator comes and releases unbelievably toxic substances into the air of their homes. Six to eight hours later, they return, thinking that their home is safe and pest free, when in reality you're treading into potentially dangerous territory.

Pesticide bombs contaminate every single thing in your home: your furniture, your carpeting, your clothes, your plants, your pets. Exterminator bombs have a lasting impact on your indoor environment, too, since the pesticides they contain—mainly pyrethrums, which induce nausea, wheezing, and skin allergies—do not disperse to the outside. Instead, they linger inside your home for weeks afterward. Repeated exposure can contribute to permanent scarring, reproductive problems, and—from the evidence of recent animal studies—possibly even cancer.

The ultimate irony is that these toxic pesticide bombs don't even work very well. In one of my first New York City apartments, I remember, my landlord regularly sent an exterminator over to roach-bomb the place. We'd come home to horrible, toxic smells—and the roaches would still be there! They might stay away for a week at most, but they'd always be back, more numerous than ever. Some apartment buildings are roach-bombed every single month, always with the same disappointing results, not to mention the toxic buildup in the reproductive system of males and females.

And when you use pesticides recklessly, you're also setting off a chain reaction of tragedies in your ecosystem. Say you spread poison on your lawn to kill off some ants. After those ants die, another larger critter will come along to eat them—and just like that, your lawn poison has entered the food chain. Before too long, bears and other large animals are being exposed to the chemicals that you thoughtlessly threw on your lawn.

As a culture, we need to start considering the big picture, instead of being so myopic about what we want at any given moment. Part of living green involves taking responsibility for our actions. We need to give more thought to how our most minor decisions can shape, for better or worse, the world around us.

Integrated Pest Management

To keep pests out of your home, the best defense is a good offense. I always tell people to practice integrated pest management, or IPM. IPM specialists control outbreaks of pests not with chemicals, but with much safer mechanical and physical techniques.

When you first move into a home or apartment, hire an IPM expert to survey every crevice, hole, and crack in your walls, floors, and ceilings. There are lots of spots—cracks in the baseboards, the intersection of the floor and walls, air-conditioning vents, those little crevices behind the pipes underneath your kitchen sink—that critters can use to enter your home without your knowledge. The IPM specialist will seal off these holes by filling them with steel wool, which is obviously nontoxic. The IPM guy will also put tiny woven mesh grilles behind the air-conditioning and heating vents to keep out the rodents.

If you take these simple measures early on, chances are you'll prevent any major infestations in the future. And though you might have to spend a little money up front on IPM, in the long run you'll save big on exterminating costs. There are other easy steps you can take to fight off pests on a day-by-day basis:

• Clean up food spills immediately. Make sure that pests can never get anywhere near your food.

• Keep all garbage cans tightly closed, and take out the trash daily.

• Keep hard-to-reach areas clean and dust-free. Regularly remove the clutter where pests can hide, particularly in your closets. Store out-of-season clothes in paper or cardboard boxes sealed against moths.

• Store foods attractive to pests, such as flour, in the refrigerator. Cereals and other pantry items should be kept in tightly sealed containers.

• Because water attracts pests, repair leaky faucets or pipes promptly.

• Screen your doors and windows and the area behind your air-conditioning and heating vents.

For more comprehensive information on nontoxic pest-control strategies, visit www.beyondpesticides.com. The Web site www.pestproductsonline .com also has a great selection of organic pest-control solutions. Eco-Safety Products (www.ecosafetyproducts.com) also has a number of natural pest-control solutions.

Roaches

Of all household pests, roaches are the hardest to control—and they're also the most dangerous to live around. Many people are allergic to the dust roaches carry around on their backs. Repeated exposure to it can lead to asthma and other respiratory problems. In low-income areas with horrible roach infestations, the rates of asthma and allergies are disproportionately high.

When I asked my IPM specialist how to get rid of these stubborn creatures without toxins, he referred me to Dr. Myles Bader's *1001 All-Natural Secrets to a Pest-Free Property*, which has a lot of great tips. He recommends putting dried bay leaves in cupboards and drawers, and cucumber peels near pipes and sinks and other moist areas where roaches might enter. He also has this easy recipe for getting rid of both roaches and ants:

Combine 1 cup borax, ¼ cup crushed fresh pepper, and ¼ cup crushed bay leaves in a jar. Close the lid and shake well. Place mixture in the corners of pantries and drawers, and you should never see another roach or ant again!

Like me, Dr. Bader recommends prevention as the most effective pest-control solution and provides these guidelines for making your house as unenticing as possible to roaches:

- Clean out the back of the fridge regularly, removing any foods that have been pushed behind things.

- Vacuum regularly.

- Keep your kitchen floor clean.

- Wipe down counters daily.

- Clean out your pets' food dishes daily and don't leave them out overnight.

- Keep the lid on your garbage tightly closed.

- Seal cracks and crevices; fix all leaky pipes.

- Repair any loose wallpaper—roaches love feasting on the paste!

- Make sure there's no lumber or loose foliage too close to your house.

- Remove stacks of magazines and newspapers, as roaches like to burrow in them.

For more great tips like this, I really recommend Dr. Bader's book.

Ants and Other Small Insects

Ants and other small bugs are annoying but relatively easy to manage without resorting to chemical pest control.

- Loose coffee grounds are great at repelling ants. Just sprinkle some coffee grounds around the perimeter of your floors, where the ants traditionally enter, and you'll immediately notice a difference. If you have a serious infestation, you can sprinkle the grounds all around the outside perimeter of your house as well.

• Peppermint oil and vinegar can combat ants, dust mites, and even bedbugs. Combine with distilled water in a bottle and spray where needed. Peppermint oil is very strong, so make sure that you dilute it sufficiently.

• Neem oil also repels ants.

• Cinnamon and orange will repel ants and other small insects.

• You can also sprinkle paprika, red chili pepper, and dried peppermint around your kitchen or any other affected areas.

• The Web site www.ultimatepestrepeller.com sells an electronic ant-control device.

Termites

The menace termites poses cannot be underestimated: They can completely destroy the foundation of your home. But because termites work slowly, you can easily stop them if you catch them in time. Call in a professional to check all the wood in your house. Prevention, as always, is the best cure. If you wait too long, you may find yourself facing a full-blown crisis.

Whatever you do, you want to avoid tenting your home to control a termite infestation. The chemicals used in tenting can leave a long-lasting residue on furniture, clothes, and carpeting. The gases professional termite exterminators use—including Vikane, or sulfuryl fluoride, a central-nervous-system depressant that can also lead to blood and bone disorders—can linger in the air for up to forty days. All that, and the toxic fumigants only kill the aboveground termites, not the subterranean termites that are often the source of the problem.

So instead of tenting, start with integrated pest management. An IPM specialist will be able to assess the damage the termites have done to your house. He will also be able to tell you about the new, safer options now on the market. One of these, Sentricon, is an insect-controlling bait that's installed underground. It kills termites very gradually but requires constant professional monitoring and maintenance to be effective. You can also try the Termite-Killer Paste sold by First Pest Control (www.firstpestcontrol.com). Formulated with ingredients that disrupt a termite's central nervous system, this human-safe product can kill all termites from the same nest within just ten days.

If, in the end, you find that you have no alternative to tenting, be sure to seal all your clothes and linens in airtight containers before the exterminator comes. Take rugs and linens outside to limit the contamination. And stay out of the house for as long as you can!

Rodents

The main ingredient in rat poison, warfarin, is highly toxic in concentrated form. If ingested in large amounts, warfarin can cause internal bleeding. Instead of exposing your family members to these hazards, I again suggest approaching the problem through integrated pest management.

- Make sure all holes are plugged and all vents screened. Rodents are larger than insects and easier to keep out.

• Always tightly close food containers in your kitchen. When they find nothing to eat, rodents usually lose interest.

If you still have a rodent problem, start with an old-fashioned mechanical trap. Traditional "snap" traps cost next to nothing and they work! The pest-control company Nixalite (www.nixalite.com) makes a more elaborate version of the snap trap—the Rat Zapper, which lures rodents in with dry bait and then immediately kills them using electrical energy. Rat Zappers are both more humane and less messy than mechanical traps.

Keeping Your Pets Clean and Healthy

We treat pets as valued family members, sometimes even referring to them as our children. Every year, more and more of us welcome domestic animals, especially dogs and cats, into our home. According to the American Pet Products Manufacturers Association 2005–2006 survey of national pet trends, Americans owned an estimated 90.5 million cats and 73.9 million dogs in 2004, up from 65 million. That means a significant number of U.S. households include a dog or cat.

Because we love our furry critters so much, we spend a tremendous amount of money taking care of them—$34.4 billion dollars in 2004, a figure that has almost doubled over the past decade. The pet-care industry, in other words, is hugely profitable—and powerful. Like cleaning-products manufacturers, the makers of pet products dupe us into buying a million specialty items that are not only unnecessary, but dangerous. Resist the pressure from Madison Avenue and focus instead on your pet's health.

Our pets are far more vulnerable to chemical exposures than we are. Dogs and cats, like young children, are small in size and travel close to the ground, where they're more likely to encounter toxic gases, bacteria, and other hazardous particulate matter. Think about what the average dog breathes in on the streets of New York on an average day: he's at the same level as the exhaust pipes of cars, buses, and trucks.

Grooming

Rather than add to our pets' chemical burden by washing them with toxic shampoos and placing toxic flea collars around their necks, we should concentrate on reducing their chemical burden. For starters, never take your pet to a groomer who uses toxic grooming products. If you do, you're literally sending your animal off to be poisoned for the day. When you bring that animal home, you and your children will be petting it and hugging it and breathing in all those toxins from the chemical shampoos. If your groomer refuses to give up toxic products, get another groomer. Do some Internet research for a groomer in your neighborhood who uses nontoxic products to clean your pet. For the same amount of money, you'll be doing your pet—and your family—a big favor.

When I shampoo my dog, I use the same organic shampoo that my son and husband and I use on our own hair: Avalon Organics, Aubrey Organics, or John Masters Organics. These great-smelling, healthy products all contain essential oils. For my dog, I especially like the formulas that contain ylang-ylang, which is a natural bug repellant. Other shampoo ingredients that will help to keep away pests include sage, lemongrass, eucalyptus, and rosemary.

Flea Prevention

Traditional flea collars might contain organophosphates and other hazardous insecticides. These chemicals "leak out" over the course of several months, keeping fleas and ticks at bay. Unfortunately, it isn't just the insects that are coming into contact with the dangerous pesticides found in flea collars. It's also your pets—and your kids. Think about it: every time your kids pet your dog or cat, they might well be exposing themselves to the pesticides in the flea collar.

There are safer ways to keep fleas off your animals. You can start by bathing them with the essential oil-based shampoos that I recommend above. Our Norfolk terrier, Virgil, runs around the ranch all summer long and never has a problem with fleas. You can also try looking for a nontoxic plant- and essential-oil-based flea collar that will protect your pet from fleas without damaging your animal or your children.

I also recommend adding garlic to your dog's diet. You can put garlic in either a dehydrated powder or flake form directly to the dog's food, or you can wrap up a pill in a little piece of soy cheese. These two supplements—brewer's yeast and garlic—not only repel fleas; they add shine to your dog's coat and boost the immune system. Essential oils can also help: putting some eucalyptus near your pet's sleeping area will also work to fend off the fleas.

Chapter 9

The Laundry Room

The Art of Laundry

Doing laundry is a fundamental household activity, and yet most of us relegate the laundry area to a dank, dark corner of the house—in the back of the kitchen or underneath exposed pipes in the basement. But your laundry room shouldn't be an afterthought, a cramped, unpleasant space that you try to escape as quickly as possible. It should be a clean, inviting atmosphere.

It doesn't take money to make the place where you do laundry pleasant. All it takes is a little imagination—and pride. Even if you live in an apartment or small home with limited space, you should make an effort to do your laundry in the cleanest, healthiest setting possible. After all, we probably spend eight to twelve hours a week doing laundry. I'd wager that most of us spend more time, on average, in the laundry room than in our elaborately decorated dining rooms.

Laundry shouldn't be a dreaded chore. Since we can't get out of washing our clothes, we might as well enjoy the process. Other cultures, like the French and Chinese, have turned the daily necessity of washing and folding shirts into an art form, and we should, too. Devoting more time to the basics in life—like setting a table with pretty napkins and fresh-cut flowers instead of wolfing down dinner in front of the television with no family conversation—elevates the whole nature of the experience.

Washing a bunch of towels should be no different. It just makes common sense to clean your clothes in a clean environment. When I designed my home, creating a pleasant laundry room was high on my list of priorities. I put the room on the second floor, not hidden away in the basement. It's not a large room, just big enough for a washer, dryer, beautiful counters where I fold the clothes, and cabinets where I can keep cleaning products and other relevant supplies and tools. On the floor, instead of unfinished concrete I used nontoxic cork, which absorbs sound and keeps the room nice and quiet even when the dryer is running. I also have drying racks for sweaters and lingerie, an area for hand-washing with a slop sink and drain, and several big stainless-steel buckets for soaking clothes.

Avoiding chemical products is a fundamental part of making your laundry room into a pleasant physical environment that encourages, not inhibits, cleaning. Instead of toxins and synthetic fragrances, you'll be breathing in essential oils and natural fragrances that will enhance your mood and boost your spirits.

The Basics: Washing and Drying

On a daily basis, the average American home can use as much electricity as a small business or even a small industrial plant. Between plug-in toasters, computers, televisions, washer-dryers, dishwashers, alarm clocks, hair dryers, blenders, coffee makers, and all the other appliances in our homes, we're completely dependent on coal, petroleum, and electricity. We've become so technology crazed that most of us don't even consider the environmental impact of running our washing machines and dryers several times a day. We wear clothes once, sometimes for just a few hours, and then throw them into the washing machine. These practices are bad for our clothing, which wears out more quickly. They're also expensive and wasteful, and can add hundreds of dollars to our electricity bills every year.

❋ Tip: If you're in the market for a new washing machine, dryer, or any other major household appliance, try looking for one with the Energy Star label. Energy Star machines use much less energy than traditional machines, and they're much easier on the environment.

Spotlight on: Laundry Detergents

We spend the majority of our time in clothes, so why don't we pay more attention to the products we use to wash them? Most commercial laundry detergents on the market today contain harmful chemicals that can aggravate our respiratory systems and cause serious hormonal dysfunction.[*]

These products may contain:

- Alkylphenolic compounds
- Artificial fragrances
- Chlorine bleach
- EDTA
- Optical brighteners is a generic term for the synthetic chemicals used in laundry detergents to make clothes appear "whiter." These nonbiodegradable substances, which are toxic to fish, do

---

[*] For detailed information on these toxins, please refer to the Glossary of Chemicals on p. 203 as well as the alkylphenolic Toxic Interruption on p. 181, the chlorine bleach Toxic Interruption on p. 24, and the phenols Toxic Interruption on p. 144.

nothing to get clothes cleaner; they simply trick the eye. When exposed to sunlight, optical brighteners can provoke allergic reactions.

- Phenol
- Polycarboxylates
- Sodium hydroxide

Suggested Natural Alternatives: Instead of exposing your family to these toxins, buy a concentrated natural detergent and simply use less of it in the wash cycle. The Imus GTC line has an excellent biodegradable and nontoxic laundry liquid that's made without phosphates, fragrances, or harsh chemicals. Several other green companies make great laundry liquids, too, including Bi-O-Kleen, Ecover, and Seventh Generation. When choosing a natural detergent, make sure that it meets the following standards:

- It should not contain petroleum products
- It should be phosphate free
- It should contain no chlorine
- It should be free of synthetic toxic fragrances and dyes
- It should not contain optical brighteners

And remember, never buy any product that doesn't disclose all ingredients on the label!

Other washing machine tricks:

- Add a cup of vinegar to the wash cycle to help keep colors bright (but *do not* use vinegar with bleach, as the resulting fumes are extremely hazardous). Vinegar is also the best natural fabric softener there is.

- One-half to three-quarters of a cup of baking soda will leave clothes soft and smelling clean and fresh.

✳ **Essential Oil Tip:** I like putting a few drops of lavender, lemon, eucalyptus, or Dr. Young's Melrose blend in the washing machine during the wash cycle. The oil will brighten and disinfect your clothes, as well as adding a wonderful scent. Clove, lemon, and eucalyptus in the rinse cycle are particularly effective at getting rid of mold on towels.

Washing Machine Alternatives

Spotlight on: Magnet Balls

I've seen a lot of advertisements lately for magnet balls, touted as a new method for "dry washing," or getting your clothes clean without water. Magnet balls work by magnetically pulling the soil and dirt off clothes. But while they have great potential to shape the future of green cleaning, magnet-ball technology just isn't advanced enough yet. One study has shown magnet balls to remove, on average, less than 45 percent of dirt from clothing, roughly the same amount that clothing washed in plain water will remove. By comparison, standard detergent removes around 80 percent of soil from clothing.

Spotlight on: Silver-Ion Washing Machine

Samsung, the makers of this state-of-the-art—and still extremely expensive, at about $1,300—washer, claims that the SilverCare washing machine effectively uses silver ions to disinfect clothing and kill odor-causing bacteria, sterilizing clothes so gently that you can wash them in cold water without ever resorting to chlorine bleach. But because silver-ion machines are still so new to the market, we don't yet know how well they work. Another potential concern is that the silver ions used in the SilverCare machine are nano-sized, and scientists have not yet determined what if any impact nanoparticles have on the environment.

Magnet-ball and silver-ion washers are definitely steps in the right direction and will probably play a part in the future of green cleaning. But until the technology is proven, I think it's best to stick with an Energy Star model of a traditional washing machine. The Green Guide recommends energy-efficient front-loading washers or the new Energy Star–rated Fisher & Paykel Intuitive Eco Washer, a top-loading machine with a drum that combines the best features of top and front loaders. It also can sense the size of your load and the type of fabric it contains, then adjust the water quantities and temperatures accordingly (www.usa .fisherpaykel.com, 888-936-7872).

Hand Washing

Washing your clothes, especially your delicates, by hand is another simple way to save on laundry costs. Instead of sending my cashmere and wool sweaters to the dry cleaner, I just wash them in a little bit of nontoxic laundry liquid, preferably one with the essential oils that leave my clothes smelling so great.

To hand-wash delicates like sweaters, put a dime-size amount of nontoxic laundry liquid in a stainless steel bucket, and fill the bucket with warm water. Then just dip your sweater into the bucket a couple of times and remove. Don't wring out the sweater when you're done. Just pat it dry with a towel and then hang it on a wooden drying rack. I don't even really rinse out the laundry liquid; I just let the clothes dry with the soap still in them. Because I'm not using any phosphates or other harsh detergent additives, I'm protecting the fabrics. The sweaters come out looking new, and I've spent almost no money.

You can also use this gentle method to wash baby clothes or any fabrics that need special attention. I like to soak my son's socks and underwear overnight in one of these buckets, and his pants whenever they're stained. Even if you have a heavy-duty laundry detergent that takes the stains out, soaking the clothes overnight is a great idea.

Drying

We're so technology driven in this country. If we can't get a machine to do the job for us, we're simply not interested—even if the alternatives are easier or cheaper. Drying your clothes in a machine is fast, but it uses a tremendous amount of energy and can also compromise the integrity of your fabrics. I encourage you to explore other ways to dry your clothes.

Clotheslines: When I was growing up, we had a clothes dryer in the house, but on sunny days, especially in the summer months, my mother hung our sheets and T-shirts and underwear on this really great clothesline that my father had rigged to work on a pulley system. I used to love to stand on our big back porch while my mom hung the clothes. Afterward, when the clothes had dried, my sister and I would sit out on the porch folding the laundry and stacking it in a big basket.

I don't see many clotheslines anymore, which is a shame. If you live in a suburban or rural area and there are no municipal ordinances to stop you, why not try drying your sheets on a clothesline every once in a while? Let's bring back that great practice. In the warmer seasons, you don't have to use the dryer at all. The clothes smell wonderful afterward, and you can also significantly cut down on your ironing, since clothes hung to dry outside usually come back pretty wrinkle-free.

Wooden Drying Racks: Consider purchasing a drying rack to minimize your drying costs. When you're done using it, you can fold it up and store it anywhere. At my house, we use these convenient foldout racks to hang-dry any number of items, particularly delicate clothes that might get damaged in the dryer. In Europe, everyone—no matter how rich or poor—has one of these racks. They take up no space, cost about $20, and are great for drying your smaller loads.

Softening Fabrics

Spotlight on: Fabric Softeners and Dryer Sheets

Traditional fabric softeners and dryer sheets—which are meant to impart a pleasant scent to your fabrics and keep them from stiffening—contain some pretty scary ingredients. What's more, these products are absolutely unnecessary. When washing your clothes with nontoxic laundry liquid, you can just add vinegar to the rinse cycle—it's the healthiest and most economical way to keep your fabrics soft.*

These products may contain:
- Benzyl acetate
- Limonene
- Linalool
- Phenol
- Phosphoric acid

Suggested Natural Alternatives:
- Distilled white vinegar, preferably organic, is the best and healthiest softener. Just put a tablespoon in the rinse cycle, as you would any of

---

*For more detailed information on these toxins, please refer to the Glossary of Chemicals on p. 203 as well as the phenols Toxic Interruption on p. 144.

the toxic fabric softeners. (Don't overdo it—you don't want your clothes to smell like vinegar!) Your clothes will come out soft every time.

- **Baking soda** is great at softening fabrics, especially in areas with hard water. For best results, add a quarter of a cup to the wash cycle.

❋ **Essential Oil Tip:** For fragrance, try adding a few drops of essential oil to your rinse cycle: fir, spruce, lavender, cedarwood, wintergreen, and rosewood all leave your clothes smelling great. As an alternative to dryer sheets, place a washcloth with ten drops of lavender, lemon, tea tree, or bergamot oil into the dryer. While they won't reduce static cling, essential oils will give a fresh, natural scent to your laundry.

Stain and Spot Removal

Spotlight on: Stain Removers

Beware of commercial stain and spot removers. They are highly toxic, associated with many acute and chronic health effects. As long as you treat your clothes soon after soiling them, you should have no problem getting the stains out naturally. The organic solvents that many formulas contain are major groundwater contaminants. Other ingredients in stain removers might cause cancer.*

These products may contain:
- Benzene
- Perchlorethylene (PERC)
- Trichlorethane (TCA)

*For detailed information on these toxins, please refer to the Glossary of Chemicals on p. 203 as well as the petroleum distillates Toxic Interruption on p. 58.

Suggested Natural Alternatives:

- When I have a stain, I usually just soak my soiled clothes in non-toxic laundry liquid for at least half an hour before washing.

- You can also try making a paste out of baking soda, applying it to the clothes, and then letting it set for an hour before washing it.

- Lemon juice, which contains citric acid, is often effective at lightening stains, especially on white fabrics. It can also work as a mild lightener or natural bleach when used with sunlight. Just make a paste of lemon juice and baking soda and leave it on the stain for at least half an hour before washing. This works really well on sweat stains in particular.

- Watered-down hydrogen peroxide also removes tough stains from white fabrics. It can get blood out of sheets. Just make sure that you dilute the hydrogen peroxide thoroughly. If in too concentrated a form, it can destroy the integrity of the fabric.

- You can find a good selection of healthy green products in stores now. Ecover makes an effective spot and stain remover, and Bi-O-Kleen makes a great enzyme stain treatment.

- Commercial dry cleaning can actually make a stain worse by setting it. Before taking stained clothing to the dry cleaner, you should try one of these tricks first.

Ironing and Starching

When you first bring home your new iron, make sure that you read the enclosed instructions so that you know how to use it correctly. Instead of purified or distilled water, many people fill their irons with tap water, which contains minerals that can damage the iron. If you iron a delicate fabric at too high a temperature, the fabric will melt and stick to the end of your iron. At this point, you'll probably try to scrub off the fabric residue, unknowingly removing the coating from the bottom of your iron in the process. When at last your mistreated iron stops working, rather than get it repaired, you'll probably send it off to the landfill and buy a new one. Most irons contain mercury, lead, cadmium, and other heavy metals, all of which contribute to our global warming problem. So, for the sake of the planet, learn how to take care of your iron.

✳ **Product Recommendation:** Lifekind (www.lifekind.com) makes an organic ironing-board cover and pad that will keep ironing chemicals from seeping into your clothing.

Spotlight on: Spray Starch

I grew up ironing. My sister and I washed and ironed all of our clothes for ourselves. Almost every night, we would iron the uniform shirts and skirts that we'd wear to school the next day. We never used starch on any of our clothes, and I still don't. My husband does get his button-down shirts starched, and cowboys at the ranch starch their jeans. But however often you starch your clothes, try to avoid using commercial spray-starch products. Aside from the starch itself, which is generally cornstarch, your average can of spray starch might contain formaldehyde, a suspected carcinogen, and pentachlorophenol, a suspected teratogen. And, because most spray starches come in an aerosol spray, they can also irritate the lungs and respiratory passages.*

---

*For detailed information on these toxins, please refer to the Glossary of Chemicals on p. 203 as well as the petroleum distillates Toxic Interruption on p. 58.

These products may contain:
- Aerosol propellants
- Formaldehyde
- Phenol
- Pentachlorophenol can severely irritate or burn skin, eyes, nose, mouth, throat, and lungs. Exposure to this suspected teratogen can cause headache, sweating, weakness, and trouble breathing. Pentachlorophenol might also damage the liver and kidneys.

Making Your Own Natural Starch

Most linen sprays—also called ironing sprays—sold in stores are loaded with artificial fragrances and phosphates. I find it's much cheaper and safer to make my own linen spray at home. It takes two minutes to mix up and really helps with the ironing. I really encourage you to try it.

1. Buy half-a-dozen or so 32-ounce spray bottles made of #1 or #2 plastic. These bottles are really useful in every room of your house, and you can buy them anywhere: at Target, Costco, Sam's Club, Linens 'n Things. In the kitchen, I even use spray bottles for spraying olive oil on food.

2. Fill the bottle almost to the top with distilled water. It's important not to use chlorinated tap water or even filtered or bottled water for this step. They all contain minerals, which can stain clothes. Just buy a big jug of distilled water and keep it in your laundry room or under the sink.

3. Add six to eight drops of your favorite essential oil to the spray bottle. You can choose from literally hundreds of different oils; over time you'll develop your personal preferences. Lavender is relaxing and helps you sleep, so it's great for bedding. A lot of women like rose, which is a more expensive oil, and for kids' rooms, grapefruit is a really popular choice.

4. On napkins and tablecloths, lemon is a really fresh, nice scent, particularly in the summer. In the winter, you can try a woodier, heavier smell like patchouli.

5. Add a little nontoxic laundry liquid—about a quarter of a teaspoon—to give the solution the right consistency. If you use just the essential oil in the distilled water, you might get spots when you spray, so it's important to include the laundry liquid.

6. Shake up the bottle and as you iron, spray it all over your clothes, linens, tablecloths, and napkins. You'll find that the spray works as a starch and actually helps get the wrinkles out.

✳ Tip: I make a couple of bottles at a time and keep them in the laundry room. One or two bottles should last you several months, depending on the size of your family. Making this solution at home will save you a lot of money and keep your fabric smelling clean and fresh without using any chemicals.

Frances Garcia's Tip

Frances Garcia, our head housekeeper at the ranch, remembers her mother and grandmother making their own clothing starch from scratch. They'd put two cups of flour, one cup of sugar, and two quarts of water in a big pot on the stove. Then they'd bring it to a boil and keep it boiling long enough to get rid of any lumps in the mixture. They'd take the shirts out of the washing machine and dip them in the pot until they were coated with the starch solution. They'd remove them and let them dry until just damp. Then, bunch up the shirts into a little ball and put them in a bag so that they'll stay damp, but not wet, until you're ready to iron them. When those shirts were ironed, they'd come out looking crisp and perfect.

Now, obviously, I'm not recommending anyone try this recipe at home. These days, there isn't a mom on the planet who has the time for such an elaborate project. I do want to remind everyone, though, that if we're creative and innovative in our cleaning, we can always come up with safe, fun alternatives. A few generations ago, people cleaned everything entirely without toxins—why have we moved so far away from those practices? By switching over to chemical cleaning products, what have we actually gained?

Dry Cleaning

Professional dry cleaning is a dirty business. Dry-cleaning workers are at a higher risk of developing certain types of cancer, in addition to other exposure-related illnesses such as liver and kidney damage. Most traditional dry-cleaning processes use perchloroethylene, or PERC, a colorless, man-made liquid that enters your home on the clothes you bring back from the dry cleaner. This highly toxic solvent evaporates in fumes in the air that you and your family members inhale. PERC can also travel through soil and contaminate groundwater, which is just one reason that families who live near dry cleaners—even if they don't take their clothes to be cleaned there—are at a higher risk of exposure. For more detailed information on alternatives to toxic dry cleaning, see Chapter 7, *The Bedroom*.

Suggested Natural Alternatives:
• Look for an environmentally responsible dry cleaner near your home. Ten years ago, it was almost impossible to find a dry cleaner who didn't use PERC, even in New York City. But these days, it's becoming increasingly common for cleaners to use nontoxic solvents and other safe dry-cleaning methods. If your cleaner does use PERC and refuses to consider less-toxic options, take your dry-cleaning business elsewhere.

• See if there are any professional "wet-cleaning" businesses in your area. Over the past decade, high-tech wet-cleaning services have emerged that clean garments without solvents or toxins. I think you will start to see more and more of these businesses in the years to come, as more of us seek out alternatives to PERC-based dry cleaning.

• When you're shopping, try to avoid buying dry-clean-only garments. Over the years, these clothes can end up costing much more to clean than you initially paid for them. Add up your dry-cleaning costs over several months and you might be surprised by how much you spend.

• Handwashing works really well on most wool and cashmere sweaters. It's also a lot gentler on your clothes than most professional dry cleaning.

Toxic Interruption
Alkylphenolics

One of the most common—and dangerous—detergent additives is alkylphenol ethoxylates (APEs), a class of chemical compounds that includes nonylphenol ethoxylates (NPEs) and octylphenol ethoxylates (OPEs). For more than fifty years, these synthetic derived surfactants have been added to detergents, disinfectants, stain removers, and degreasers, and are used in the manufacture of textiles, pulp and paper, paints, adhesives, resins, and protective coatings.

Of the 450 million pounds of alkyphenolic compounds we produce in this country every year, NPEs have given scientists particular cause for concern. These popular detergent additives have well-documented estrogenic properties, and when released into community wastewater cause great harm to aquatic life, interfering with the reproductive cycles of salmon, rainbow trout, and other fish. NPEs also take much longer to biodegrade than most cleansing agents and in fact become even *more* toxic as they break down into simpler compounds, contaminating our sewage plants and damaging aquatic life.

Given these proven threats to the environment, many European countries have banned the use of alkylphenolic compounds in domestic cleaning products—the English prohibition dates all the way back to 1976—and replaced them with the slightly more expensive and much safer alcohol ethoxylates. But while some U.S. companies have voluntarily eliminated NPEs from their cleaning products, others continue to use them in huge quantities. Until we take regulatory action to ban NPEs and other alkylphenolic compounds from household cleaning products, we will continue to put our ecosystem in grave danger.

Chapter 10

The Green Revolution

Greening is by no means a new phenomenon—it's just been getting more attention in recent years, as the toll of toxic chemicals in our environment becomes more evident. The greening movement has come a long, long way in the last decade alone. Every day, I see more advertisements for green products and articles about environmentally responsible lifestyle choices. As increasing numbers of us demand alternatives to the toxins that have ravaged our bodies for the last fifty years, more stores in more parts of the country are selling organic food and personal-care products and even organic building materials.

But while greening is on the verge of becoming mainstream, we still have a long way to go—particularly when it comes to our cleaning products. The chemical industry is completely unregulated in this country, and the makers of toxic cleaning agents don't have to answer to anyone, not even the FDA. Misleading and incomplete labels can cause us to make the wrong choices for our family.

I hope that after reading this book, you feel equipped with enough information and commonsense know-how to start cleaning up your life. And remember, you should never feel anxious when you contemplate making those first small changes—there's nothing in the world more toxic than stress. Green cleaning is incredibly easy, given all the options already out there. The increased efficiency of essential oils and nontoxic formulas made from filtered water and plant-derived ingredients means that you don't have to depend on as many products, while microfiber mops and cloths reduce the amount of water needed for cleaning. These innovations make cleaning both more efficient and more fun.

In the years to come, I predict we'll be seeing even more creative green cleaning solutions. As a larger population of educated consumers rejects toxic cleaning products, green alternatives will become even more available, and at lower prices. At the same time, essential oil–based germicides and disinfectants will gain acceptance, and it will one day be standard to use filtered water in *all* cleaning products. Instead of dangerous pesticides on our lawns, we'll be using more microbes and "good" bacteria that maintain the balance of our ecosystem. We'll start choosing building materials based on their efficiency and safety— low-maintenance, nontoxic cork and rubber flooring, for example, will one day replace wall-to-wall carpeting.

With the serious environmental problems our industrialized society is facing, we must continue to experiment with new green cleaning technologies. We'll be seeing the use of zeolites, or volcanic ash, to remove toxic heavy metals from our increasingly polluted indoor air. And as we enter an era when water is a precious resource, there will be a greater demand for efficient, waterless cleaning alternatives, like magnetic ions, particularly in areas affected by droughts.

There really is a green revolution on the horizon. One day—and I hope not too long from now—the major toxic cleaning-product corporations will be forced to phase out the chemicals, replacing them with healthier, sustainable ingredients that don't bioaccumulate in the environment *or* in our bodies. Sooner than we realize, all schools, hospitals, corporations, and government agencies will implement green cleaning programs for the safety of our health and our environment.

In the meantime, you can start your own little revolution today, right inside your home. Make a commitment, as I did, to improve the quality of your life. Exercise, eat and sleep well, don't smoke or drink. Become aware of the impact your actions have on the whole environment, and try to act on that sense of responsibility. As a culture, I think we're all longing to live closer to nature, to be cleaner and healthier, to give our children a more nurturing environment. Green cleaning is a great tool on that journey—good luck!

three:
resources

Green Cleaning

All over the country, safe, effective natural alternatives to conventional household cleaning products are becoming more available every day. As more and more of us clean up our lives, green alternatives will be even easier to find—and cheaper, too. Look for products that disclose all ingredients (and tell you that they do).

The following recommendations are not intended to be an exclusive list—it's constantly growing and evolving, as more nontoxic cleaners hit the shelves of stores and supermarkets. Obviously, some of these products work better than others. You just have to experiment and see what you like best. All of these product lines meet my guidelines for the lowest level of toxicity possible:

Imus GTC Institutional and Retail Product Line

One hundred percent of the profits from sales of my products go to the Imus Cattle Ranch for Kids with Cancer. You can purchase products from my retail line—GTC (greening the cleaning) laundry liquid, hand dishwashing liquid, Citrus Sage All-Purpose Cleaner, Citrus Sage Glass and Window Cleaner—at www.imusranchfoods.com and at thousands of stores all over the country. For more information on the institutional line, please visit my environmental center at www.dienviro.com, or call 201-336-8071.

Bi-O-Kleen

You can buy Bi-O-Kleen's great products by visiting www.bi-o-kleen.com or calling 800-477-0188. They make everything from stain remover to produce wash. Their enzyme treatment for stains is one of my favorite products. If I didn't have a line of my own, I'd buy all Bi-O-Kleen.

Ecover

In business since 1980, Ecover (www.ecover.com) is one of the original players in the green cleaning market. You can find Ecover's diverse line of products—toilet bowl cleaner, stain remover, hand dishwashing liquid—at most health food markets and mid-size grocery stores.

Earth Friendly

Earth Friendly Products are available for purchase at www.ecos.com. This environmentally responsible company makes cleaners for every room in the house, as well as lines of personal-care and pet-care products.

Seventh Generation

Seventh Generation (www.seventhgeneration.com) has a diverse range of cleaning products—from hand dishwashing liquid and automatic dishwashing detergent to shower and toilet bowl cleaners—that are sold in grocery stores all over the country. They also make household paper products without chlorine bleach.

Sun and Earth

Sun and Earth (www.sunandearth.com) makes products for the kitchen, bathroom, and laundry room. They also sell microfiber cloths for glass and other surfaces.

Planet

Planet (www.planetinc.com) has a nice selection of nontoxic household products: all-purpose cleaner, liquid and powder laundry detergents, paper towels and toilet paper made without chlorine bleach.

Specialty Products

Williamsville Wax (call 800-453-4781 for ordering information) is a great substitute for toxic furniture polishes and waxes.

Eucalan (www.eucalan.com) makes an essential oil–based delicate wash that I use on my sweaters and other items.

Retailers

You'll increasingly find green cleaning products at your local supermarket chain, as well as any health food market in your area. These are just a few examples of retailers that sell environmentally friendly household cleaners:

Health Food Stores

Wild Oats
Wild Oats Natural Marketplace (www.wildoats.com) has over one hundred stores across North America. Expect to find a great selection of natural cleaning products.

Whole Foods
There are now 189 Whole Foods stores (www.wholefoodsmarket.com) in the U.S. and United Kingdom, and more are opening up every year.

Vitamin World
Vitamin World (www.vitaminworld.com), with locations all over the country, is another great place to find nontoxic household cleaners.

Local Health Food Markets
These days, even small health food stores will carry a selection of nontoxic household cleaners. If you have a product you already like that's not in stock, many independent retailers will special-order it for you.

Home Stores

You can find nontoxic cleaners in home furnishings and home improvement stores, too. These stores will carry many of your essential household cleaning supplies as well: microfiber mops, cloths, stainless-steel buckets . . . everything you need to get started.

Bed Bath & Beyond

Bed Bath & Beyond (www.bedbathandbeyond.com) has 725 stores nationwide, so look for one in your neighborhood.

Linens 'n Things

Linens 'n Things (www.lnt.com) are also all over the place: they have 540 stores in 47 states.

Home Improvement Stores

Some big-box home improvement or do-it-yourself retailers will have a good selection of nontoxic household products.

Supermarket Chains

More than ever, big supermarket chains are making room on their shelves for basic nontoxic cleaning products. The selection gets more extensive every day!

Web Sites

The Web is an invaluable resource for natural products of every description. If you're looking for a specific product, you can use Google.com to compare prices and availability at a wide range of online retailers. I regularly visit a number of Web sites for different household needs.

Gaiam (www.gaiam.com) sells a great selection of dechlorinators, organic shower curtains, organic cotton sheets and towels, and many other reasonably priced natural-living products. Lifekind (www.lifekind.com) also carries many excellent organic cotton products, among other great green household necessities. You can buy organic sheets and other linens at Coyuchi Organic (www. coyuchiorganic.com).

For essential oils, I go to Dr. Young's Web site (www.youngliving.com). For essential oil nebulizers and other accessories, I'm a big fan of the online retailer Abundant Health (www.abundanthealth4u.com).

If you start exploring the Web for green products, you'll find your own favorite sites to revisit again and again.

Reading Labels

When shopping for green cleaning products, you should always pay close attention to the label. If you can answer "yes" to the following questions, then you can trust that the product you're buying is safe.

Does It Disclose All Ingredients?

Because the manufacturers of household cleaning products aren't required by law to do so, you should look for companies that voluntarily disclose their ingredients—and tell you that they do. Look for products that say right on the bottle "We disclose all ingredients." That line is a good indication that you're dealing with an environmentally responsible company.

Does It Tell You Where Those Ingredients Come From?

The label should also tell you if its ingredients are synthetic or naturally derived, as in the label of this environmentally safe all-purpose product:

"This product contains purified water, naturally derived surfactant (from plants or botanicals such as corn, soy, or palm kernel), natural fragrance (from essential oils, plants or botanicals), and contains no preservatives."

Is the water purified? Is the fragrance natural? Does it tell whether the surfactant is derived from plants or chemicals? These are the questions you need to start asking.

Depending on the product, there might be a few more ingredients listed as well, like a complexing agent or a chealant. That's fine—as long as the label tells you the *source* of those ingredients, whether they're synthetic or plant-/vegetable-based.

You might also see words like "anionic," "nonionic," and "cationic" preceding the surfactant. These refer to the *charge* of the surfactant and not its source. Don't be fooled by these and other scientific-sounding terms. You need to know where that surfactant comes from, not what its charge is.

Beware of vague-sounding phrases like "quality control ingredients" or "cleaning agents." What do these words even *mean*? Do they indicate the source of the ingredients or not? If you can't answer these simple questions, you probably shouldn't be using the product.

Do Those Ingredients Biodegrade?
A label should tell you if its ingredients biodegrade in the environment. Most plant- and vegetable-based formulas do.

Is It Free of Toxins?
Avoid cleaning products that contain any of the following:

- Aerosol propellants
- Ammonia
- Chlorine bleach
- Heavy metals
- Known or suspected carcinogens, endocrine disrupters, mutagens, and teratogens
- Petroleum distillates
- Phosphates
- Synthetic dyes, fragrances, and optical brighteners

If you see any of these items on a product label, keep shopping.

General Terms Used in This Book

A **carcinogen** is any substance that can cause or aggravate cancer. Many popular cleaning products—all-purpose cleaners, dishwashing liquids, furniture polish, oven cleaners, window cleaners, air fresheners, spray starch, flea and roach bombs, and spot removers—might contain ingredients with known or suspected carcinogenic properties.

A **neurotoxin** is any poisonous chemical that acts on the body's brain and nervous system. Neurotoxins, which can affect cognitive function, have been linked to reduced IQs in children. Known neurotoxins are found in some air fresheners, disinfectants, spot removers, and permanent press fabrics. Other known neurotoxins are mercury and manganese.

A **mutagen** is any agent that causes a permanent genetic change in a cell. The term **mutagenicity** refers to the capacity of a chemical or physical agent to bring about this unnatural permanent alteration. Phenol, an ingredient in some spray starches, laundry detergents, all-purpose cleaners, air fresheners, disinfectants, and furniture polish, is both a mutagen and a suspected carcinogen.

Endocrine disrupters can be naturally occurring hormones or manmade chemicals that may interfere with the body's hormonal or reproductive system. Endocrine disrupters can mimic, block, or interfere with natural hormones, causing all sorts of problems to develop, including altered immune function, developmental disabilities, and endometriosis. Some laundry detergents, furniture waxes, and metal polishes might all contain endocrine disrupters, which can also be referred to as hormone mimics, hormone disrupters, or reproductive disrupters.

Teratogens are substances that interfere with fetal development, causing malformation or serious deviation from normal development of embryos and fetuses. Some glass cleaners, all-purpose cleaners, and spray starches all might contain teratogens.

Toxic chemicals, or **toxins,** are substances that can cause severe illness, poisoning, birth defects, disease, or death when ingested, inhaled, or absorbed by living organisms. A **toxic substance** is a chemical or mixture that can cause illness, death, disease, or birth defects. The quantities and exposures necessary to cause these effects can vary widely. Many toxic substances are pollutants and contaminants in the environment.

A **toxic cloud** is a plume of airborne gases, vapors, fumes, or aerosols containing toxic materials.

Toxic pollutants are substances that can harm the environment or cause death, disease, or birth defects in the organisms that ingest or absorb them. The quantities and length of exposure necessary to cause these effects can vary widely.

Toxic waste is waste that can produce injury if inhaled, swallowed, or absorbed through the skin.

Volatile organic compounds are substances containing carbon and different proportions of other elements such as hydrogen, oxygen, fluorine, chlorine, bromine, sulfur, or nitrogen; these substances easily become vapor or gases. A significant number of VOCs are commonly used as solvents (paint thinners, lacquer thinners, degreasers, and dry cleaning fluids).

A **biodegradable** substance is one capable of being broken down by living things like microorganisms and bacteria and fungi, then absorbed into the ecosystem. A "readily biodegradable" substance will be quickly decomposed into harmless by-products, while an "inherently biodegradable" substance will eventually biodegrade over time.

Waterborne contaminants are unhealthy chemicals, microorganisms (like bacteria), or radiation, found in tap water.

Persistent bioaccumulative toxins, or PBTs, are compounds that, once introduced, "persist" in the environment. A compound may persist for less than a second or indefinitely, for tens or thousands of years. A bioaccumulative substance is one that increases in concentration in living organisms over time. When toxins bioaccumulate in the fatty tissues of our bodies and enter the food chain, they can cause serious long-term health problems and even alter our genetic makeup permanently.

Petrochemicals are intermediate chemicals derived from petroleum, hydrocarbon liquids, or natural gas.

Glossary of Chemicals

All of the chemicals I've listed below have been shown to be actual or potential hazards to humans or the environment. Whether, and to what extent, these are dangerous in any specific situation depends on a variety of factors, such as: means of exposure (skin contact, inhalation, ingestion); how much was she exposed to; over how long a time was she exposed to it; was she exposed to it in combination with other chemicals. One brief contact with a single item that was washed with chlorine bleach may have no long-lasting health effects. However, immersing delicate skin in it for an extended period of time will almost certainly have ill effects, and drinking a bottle of it will probably be lethal. I firmly believe that knowing all of the potential toxins in home products is the only way to ensure the safety of you, your family, and the environment.

Aerosol propellants—including isobutene, butane, and propane—are eye, throat, and respiratory irritants that aggravate asthma and cause other lung diseases. Exposure to aerosol propellants can also lead to eye injuries and chemical burns.

Cleaning products that might contain **aerosol propellants:** oven cleaners, carpet cleaners, furniture polishes and waxes, air fresheners, insecticides, upholstery cleaners, spray starches.

Alkylphenolic compounds, including APEs and NPEs, are synthetic surfactants that do not readily biodegrade in soil and water. They are endocrine disrupters that have been shown to mimic the hormone estrogen and disrupt the body's hormone signals that regulate reproduction and development.

Cleaning products that might contain **alkylphenolic compounds:** all-purpose cleaners, laundry detergents.

Ammonia is listed as a toxic chemical on the EPA's Community Right-to-Know list. It irritates the skin, eyes, and respiratory passages, causing all sorts of respiratory problems, including pulmonary edema. It is extremely toxic when inhaled in concentrated vapors and repeated exposure may lead to bronchitis and pneumonia. Ammonia can cause chemical burns, cataracts, and corneal damage, and has been shown to produce skin cancer.

Cleaning products that might contain **ammonia:** automatic dishwasher detergents, window cleaners, furniture polishes and waxes, metal polishes and cleaners.

Artificial fragrances are synthetic chemical blends that can irritate the skin and cause headaches, sneezing, and watery eyes. They are 95 percent derived from petroleum. Artificial fragrances might also contain toxins like methylene chloride, the preservative formaldehyde, and phthalates. Fragrances can induce or worsen respiratory problems, particularly in people with asthma, allergies, sinus problems, rhinitis, and other conditions.

Cleaning products that might contain **artificial fragrances:** all-purpose cleaners, toilet bowl cleaners, furniture polishes and waxes.

Benzene—sometimes called benzol, benzole, annulene, benzeen, phenyl hydride, and coal naphtha—is a petroleum derivative classified by the International Agency for Research on Cancer as a carcinogen. Benzene is also listed in the 1990 Clean Air Act as a hazardous air pollutant.

Cleaning products that might contain **benzene:** oven cleaners, detergents, furniture polishes and waxes, spot removers.

Butyl cellosolve—also known as 2-butoxyethanol, butyl oxitol, ethylene glycol monobutyl ether—is a suspected teratogen that can damage both developing fetuses and male reproductive glands. This synthetic solvent and grease cutter can irritate mucous membranes and cause liver and kidney damage. A known irritant to eyes, nose, throat, and mouth, butyl cellosolve is a neurotoxin that can depress the nervous system. In the short term, exposure to butyl cellosolve can cause headaches, dizziness, lightheadedness, confusion, and even loss of consciousness. Butyl cellosolve can also contribute to learning disabilities among children.

Cleaning products that might contain **butyl cellosolve:** all-purpose cleaners and degreasers, window cleaners, upholstery cleaners, and a wide range of other household cleaning products.

Camphor, a toxin that irritates nasal passages, eyes, and throat if inhaled, can easily invade body tissues. A central nervous system stimulant, camphor causes dizziness, nausea, confusion, muscle twitches, and convulsions. It is also on the EPA's Hazardous Waste list.

Cleaning products that might contain **camphor:** fabric softeners, anything with an artificial fragrance.

Chlorinated solvents are organic solvents that contain chlorine atoms.

Cleaning products that might contain **chlorinated solvents:** dry-cleaning fluids, anything in an aerosol container.

Chlorine bleach is a powerful respiratory irritant that can be fatal when inhaled. This ubiquitous toxin—also known as sodium hypochlorite, hypochlorite, hydrogen chloride, and hydrochloric acid—is responsible for the most household poisonings in the United States. Chlorine, a prime cause of atmospheric ozone loss, is listed in the 1990 Clean Air Act as a hazardous air pollutant.

Cleaning products that might contain **chlorine bleach:** toilet bowl cleaners, laundry detergents, dishwasher detergents, tub and tile cleaners.

Chlorine dioxide. See **Chlorine bleach.**

Chloroform is a neurotoxin that can damage the central nervous system. In extreme cases, exposure to chloroform can cause cancer, heart problems, liver and kidney damage, even death. Other symptoms include dizziness, nausea, drowsiness, and respiratory problems.

Cleaning products that might contain **chloroform:** fabric softeners.

Colors and dyes are artificial colors—found on labels as FD&C or D&C and followed by a color and a number—made from petroleum and coal tar. Some are believed to cause cancer. They may penetrate the skin, cause allergies or irritate the skin and eyes. Yellow, amber, green, or blue products are obviously dyed with synthetic colors, and should be avoided.

Cleaning products that might contain **colors and dyes:** all-purpose cleaners, hand dishwashing liquids, fabric softeners.

Crystalline silica is a carcinogenic eye, skin, and lung irritant.

Cleaning products that might contain **crystalline silica:** all-purpose cleaners.

Diethanolamine (DEA) is a group of synthetic surfactants used to neutralize acids. Diethanolamines are slow to biodegrade and react with natural nitrogen oxides and sodium nitrite pollutants in the atmosphere to form nitrosamines, a family of potent carcinogens.

Cleaning products that might contain **DEA:** all-purpose cleaners, hand dishwashing liquids, many personal-care products.

Dioxane—also known as diethylene dioxide, diethylene ether, diethylene oxide—is a carcinogen listed as a hazardous air pollutant in the 1990 Clean Air Act. Dioxane—not the same thing as dioxin—is a solvent classified by the EPA as a probable human carcinogen. It may also suppress the immune system. Dioxane is on the EPA's Community Right-to-Know list.

Cleaning products that might contain **dioxane:** window cleaners.

Dioxin, the most dangerous man-made compound ever tested, has been linked to cancer and many other serious medical problems: birth defects, deformities, developmental delays, and damage to the immune, reproductive, and respiratory systems.

Cleaning products that might contain **dioxin:** anything labeled "antibacterial" or "antimicrobial" might expose you to this hazardous toxin.

D-limonene is a skin and eye irritant.

Cleaning products that might contain **D-limonene:** fabric softeners, some all-purpose cleaners.

EDTA, or ethylenediaminetetraacetate, is class of synthetic phosphate alternatives. EDTA compounds don't readily biodegrade in the environment.

Cleaning products that might contain **EDTA:** laundry detergents.

Ethylacetate is a narcotic that can cause stupor, headaches, and problems with the eyes and respiratory system. It is also on the EPA's Hazardous Waste list.

Cleaning products that might contain **ethylacetate:** fabric softeners.

Formaldehyde, a known carcinogen in humans, can severely irritate or burn skin, eyes, nose, mouth, throat, and lungs. Exposure to formaldehyde can lead to skin allergies, asthma attacks, and even pulmonary edema.

Cleaning products that might contain **formaldehyde:** air fresheners, disinfectants, spray starches.

Germicides are usually synthetic compounds that kill the microorganisms and bacteria that cause disease.

Hydrochloric acid can dissolve and destroy tender tissues upon direct contact. Its vapors irritate the eyes, nose, and throat. Hydrochloric acid can also burn, resulting in permanent scarring and even blindness.

Cleaning products that might contain **hydrochloric acid:** toilet bowl cleaners, aluminum cleaners, rust removers, oven cleaners.

Hydrofluoric acid is a common ingredient in aluminum cleaners. This corrosive toxin can burn your skin and cause blindness. It is also a major air pollutant.

Cleaning products that might contain **hydrofluoric acid:** metal cleaners and polishes.

Isopropyl alcohol can irritate skin and eyes and cause itching, redness, rash, drying, and cracking. Overexposure can cause headaches, drowsiness, confusion, lack of coordination, unconsciousness, and death. While isopropyl alcohol has not yet been adequately evaluated to determine whether repeated exposure to it can cause brain or other nerve damage, many solvents and other petroleum-based chemicals have been associated with such damage.

Cleaning products that might contain **isopropyl alcohol:** window cleaners.

Kerosene is a petroleum distillate that can damage the lungs and erode the fatty tissue that protects our nerve cells.

Cleaning products that might contain **kerosene:** furniture polishes and waxes.

Linalool is a narcotic linked to central nervous system disorders.
Cleaning products that might contain **linalool:** fabric softeners.

Methanol, or methyl alcohol, is a neurotoxin and a severe eye and skin irritant that can cause blindness.
Cleaning products that might contain **methanol:** window cleaners.

Methylene chloride is an organic chlorinated solvent and a suspected human carcinogen.
Cleaning products that might contain **methylene chloride:** air fresheners, any other artificially fragranced item.

Morpholine is an extremely toxic chemical that irritates the skin, eyes, and mucous membranes. Morpholine, which may cause liver and kidney damage, can react with nitrites to form carcinogenic nitrosamines.
Cleaning products that might contain **morpholine:** all-purpose cleaners, furniture polishes and waxes.

Naphthalene is a suspected human carcinogen that is especially harmful to small children. An eye and skin irritant, naphthalene can cause cataracts, corneal damage, kidney damage, blood damage to the fetus, and central nervous system damage. Naphthalene can also promote the breakdown of red blood cells and lead to hemolytic anemia.
Cleaning products that might contain **naphthalene:** mothballs, air fresheners, deodorizers, carpet cleaners, toilet bowl cleaners.

Naphthas. See **Petroleum distillates.**

Optical brighteners is a generic term for the synthetic chemicals used in laundry detergents to make clothes appear "whiter." These non-biodegradable substances, which are toxic to fish, do nothing to get clothes cleaner; they simply trick the eye. When exposed to sunlight, optical brighteners can provoke allergic reactions.

Cleaning products that might contain **optical brighteners:** laundry detergents.

Organic solvents are petroleum-derived neurotoxins and nervous system depressants. They're responsible for most of the groundwater pollution in this country.

Cleaning products that might contain **organic solvents:** metal polishes and cleaners, dry-cleaning fluids, all-purpose cleaners.

Oxalic acid is a gastrointestinal irritant that can be fatal in large doses. The body partially metabolizes ethylene glycol into oxalic acid.

Cleaning products that might contain **oxalic acid:** metal polishes and cleaners.

Paradichlorobenzene—also known as p-dichlorobenzene, PDCB, and 1,4-dichlorobenzene—is an extremely toxic, volatile carcinogen and endocrine disrupter that causes liver and kidney damage. Its vapors can irritate the skin, eyes, and respiratory tract. Paradichlorobenzene does not biodegrade.

Cleaning products that might contain **paradichlorobenzene:** moth repellents, toilet deodorizers, air fresheners, insecticides.

Pentachlorophenol can severely irritate or burn skin, eyes, nose, mouth, throat, and lungs. Exposure to this suspected teratogen can cause headache, sweating, weakness, and trouble breathing. Pentachlorophenol might also damage the liver and kidneys.

Cleaning products that might contain **pentachlorophenol:** spray starch.

Perchlorethylene, or **PERC,** is a man-made organic solvent and a huge groundwater contaminant. Repeated contact with PERC can remove the skin's natural protective oils, causing irritation, dryness, cracking, and dermatitis. PERC vapors can irritate the eyes, nose, and throat, causing burning and coughing. Exposure to PERC can damage the liver, kidneys, and central nervous system, and it has been shown to cause cancer in lab animals. When inhaled by a pregnant woman, it can interfere with a developing fetus and also contaminate breast milk.

Cleaning products that might contain **PERC:** spot removers, degreasers, carpet cleaners, dry-cleaning fluids.

Petroleum distillates, also called hydrocarbons, naphthas, or petrochemicals, are found in the vast majority of commercial cleaning products. We're *way* too dependent on petroleum in this country, and it's killing our kids—and the environment. Petroleum products are suspected human carcinogens responsible for atmospheric emissions that contribute to global warming. Petroleum distillates are neurotoxins and endocrine disrupters that accumulate in our bodies and contaminate our blood. They can damage our immune, cardiovascular, reproductive, and respiratory systems.

Cleaning products that might contain **petroleum distillates:** anything with artificial fragrance, hand dishwashing liquid, bathroom floor cleaners, air fresheners, toilet bowl deodorizers, metal polishes and cleaners.

Phenol—also known as alkyl phenoxy polyethoxy ethanol, nonyl phenoxy ethoxylate—is highly toxic, a known mutagen and suspected carcinogen. It can severely irritate or burn skin, eyes, nose, mouth, throat, and lungs. Phenol can also interfere with the ability of the blood to carry oxygen and cause bronchitis to develop. Higher exposures can cause a build-up of fluid in the lungs, which can lead to pulmonary edema. Internal consumption can lead to circulatory collapse, convulsions, cold sweats, coma, and death.

Cleaning products that might contain **phenol:** laundry detergents, all-purpose cleaners, air fresheners, disinfectants, furniture polish, metal polishes and cleaners, fabric softeners.

Phosphates, or "builders," are a major water pollutant. When built up in streams and lakes, these water-softening mineral additives encourage the overgrowth of algae and other aquatic plant life, which eventually depletes the supply of oxygen in the water and leads to the death of fish and other organisms. The use of phosphates has long since been banned in the manufacture of laundry detergents, but some automatic dishwashing detergents still incorporate them into their formula.

Cleaning products that might contain **phosphates:** dishwasher detergents, all-purpose cleaners.

Phosphoric acid is an eye, skin, and respiratory irritant featured on the EPA's Community Right-to-Know list and controlled as an air pollutant under the Clean Air Act. If inhaled, phosphoric acid vapors can make lungs burn.

Cleaning products that might contain **phosphoric acid:** toilet bowl cleaners, metal polishes and cleaners, fabric softeners.

Polycarboxylates are synthetic phosphate substitutes that have not yet been thoroughly tested for their impact on human health and the environment. These petroleum-based chemicals do not biodegrade.

Cleaning products that might contain **polycarboxylates:** automatic dishwashing detergents, laundry detergents.

Polychlorinated biphenyls (PCBs) are mixtures of 209 chemical compounds. There are no known natural sources of PCBs. PCBs are no longer manufactured in the United States, but were used in the past as flame-resistant materials, electrical insulators, heating coils, caulking compounds, and various other materials. PCBs may enter the environment during manufacture, leakage of old equipment, or leaching from landfills. PCBs are chemically stable and remain in the environment for long periods of time. Once in the environment they accumulate in the fatty tissues of animals and accumulate through the food chain. PCBs can cause serious health problems in children. Exposure during a child's developmental years can result in reduced IQ, developmental delays, attention deficit disorders, and behavioral problems.

Polyvinyl chloride, or PVC, is a raw material, used in the manufacture of everything from pacifiers and kids' toys to plastic water bottles and vinyl flooring. Made from the flammable gas vinyl chloride—a known human carcinogen that has also been linked to liver disease and other life-threatening conditions—PVCs currently represent the largest and fastest-growing use of chlorine in this country.

Propane. See **Aerosol propellants.**

Propellants. See **Aerosol propellants.**

Sodium bisulfate is corrosive and can cause asthma attacks and other respiratory problems. If swallowed, it can damage the eyes, skin, and internal tissues.
    Cleaning products that might contain **sodium bisulfate:** toilet bowl cleaners and deodorizers.

Sodium dichloroisocyanurate. See **Chlorine bleach.**

Sodium hydroxide—also known as lye, caustic soda, and soda lye—is a corrosive eye, skin, and respiratory irritant that can cause lung damage, blindness, and even death if swallowed.

Cleaning products that might contain **sodium hydroxide:** hand dishwashing liquids, automatic dishwashing detergents, laundry detergents, oven cleaners, tub and tile cleaners, toilet bowl cleaners, drain cleaners.

Sodium laureth sulfate and **sodium lauryl sulfate** are the core ingredients of most conventional hair shampoos and many other personal-care products. These synthetic surfactants can enter the bloodstream after very limited exposure and might also be "penetration enhancers," meaning they allow other chemicals to penetrate deeper into the skin.

Cleaning products that might contain **sodium laureth sulfate** and **sodium lauryl sulfate:** hand dishwashing liquids.

Sulfuric acid is a corrosive that can cause burns, eye damage, and even blindness.

Cleaning products that might contain **sulfuric acid:** drain cleaners, metal polishes and cleaners.

Synthetic pine oil can irritate eyes and mucous membranes.

Cleaning products that might contain **synthetic pine oil:** air fresheners, bathroom floor cleaners.

Thioureas are a class of organic compounds of carbon, nitrogen, sulfur, and hydrogen. Exposure to thioureas has been linked to enlarged thyroid glands and bone-marrow depression in humans. Chronic administration in rats has produced liver tumors.

Cleaning products that might contain **thioureas:** metal polishes and cleaners.

Toluene, or xylene, is a highly toxic petrochemical solvent. Like benzene, it is an aromatic solvent and a known human carcinogen. It can also affect the reproductive and central nervous systems.

Cleaning products that might contain **toluene:** stain removers.

Trichlorethane (TCA), like PERC and other organic solvents, can erode the skin's natural protective oils, causing irritation, dryness, cracking, and dermatitis. Exposure to TCA is associated with teary eyes, sore throat, nasal irritation, and coughing. At high levels, exposure to TCA can damage the liver and kidneys, and in extreme cases can cause sudden death. When inhaled by a pregnant woman, TCA can interfere with a developing fetus and also contaminate breast milk.

Cleaning products that might contain **TCA:** furniture polishes and waxes, stain removers.

Triclosan is a common disinfectant that sunlight can convert to dioxin, the most toxic substance ever tested. Triclosan is now used in a huge variety of antibacterial products, from premoistened mops to cutting boards.

Triethanolamine (TEA) is a group of synthetic surfactants that can irritate the eyes, skin, and respiratory tract. With prolonged exposure, TEA can cause permanent skin sensitization.

Cleaning products that might contain **TEA:** all-purpose cleaners, carpet cleaners.

Trisodium phosphate can irritate the skin, eyes, nose, and throat. Contact with eyes can lead to conjunctivitis, while ingestion can injure the mouth, throat, and gastrointestinal tract. Breathing the dust of trisodium phosphate may aggravate asthma or other chronic pulmonary diseases.

Cleaning products that might contain **trisodium phosphate:** all-purpose cleaners.

A Note on Sources

Throughout the book, I have relied on material from recognized scientific and government authorities. You can access many of these sources by visiting my Web site, www.dienviro.com. There you'll find topical articles, as well as links to Web sites with information on the toxins that threaten our environment—and our loved ones.

In writing this book, I've relied particularly on the following sources:

The Environmental Protection Agency

The EPA (http://epa.gov) is your first go-to source for information on toxins in the environment. The government Web site has many valuable resources, including a fact sheet entitled "Safe Substitutes at Home: Non-toxic Household Products" (http://es.epa.gov/techinfo/facts/safe-fs.html). This user-friendly Web page goes over the dangerous ingredients in many common household items and offers great suggestions for safe alternatives.

The EPA also has resources on hazardous chemicals and their effects on human health and the environment. The Emergency Planning and Community Right-to-Know Act of 1986 (http://es.epa.gov/techinfo/facts/pro-act6.html) mandated that a list of chemicals considered "extremely hazardous substances (EHS)" be made available to the public. I mention the Community Right-to-Know Act throughout the book as a broad warning: any substance that's made it onto this list is a substance you want to avoid.

Another important resource on the EPA Web site is the Toxic Release Inventory (http://www.epa.gov/tri/), a database compiled annually of the toxins released by manufacturers in certain industries. Every year, these manufacturers must disclose the quantities of approximately 350 toxic chemicals and 22 chemical categories that they release directly to air, water, or land; inject underground; or transfer to off-site facilities. The EPA compiles and makes the information available to the public under the Community Right-to-Know portion of the law. You can access more information on the inventory at www.epa.gov/tri/chemical/index.htm.

This page includes several helpful links: to the chemicals classified as carcinogens by the Occupational Safety and Health Administration (OSHA), chemical summaries released by the Agency for Toxic Substances and Disease Registry, and chemical fact sheets published by the State of New Jersey.

The EPA also includes a section known as the Terminology Reference System (http://www.epa.gov/trs/), a comprehensive guide to environmental terminology.

Environmental Health Perspectives

The National Institute of Environmental Health Sciences (www.niehs .nih.gov), one of the National Institutes of Health (www.nih.gov), has made a lot of great information available to the public. Environmental Health Perspectives (www.ehponline.org), an online journal published by the NIEHS, is a recognized, respected source of peer-reviewed articles and research that investigate "the impact of the environment on human health." I've taken facts on many different topics—VOCs, organophosphates, endocrine disrupters, phthalates, dioxin, benzene—from this journal.

The Environmental Working Group

The Environmental Working Group (www.ewg.org), a not-for-profit research and advocacy organization, publishes up-to-the-minute information on topics ranging from flame retardants to farm subsidies. It's a great source for concise, well-written articles on toxins and their impact on human health. The Web site also includes a useful reference section, "Skin Deep," which summarizes the chemical properties of ingredients in many popular health and beauty products. Several of these chemicals are the same ones found in household cleaners: http://www.ewg.org/reports/skindeep2/findings/index.php.

The Hazardless Home Handbook

The Oregon Department of Environmental Quality has made this incredibly useful A-Z guide to household hazardous substances (and ways to eliminate them) available for download. Go to www.Oregon.gov/DEQ and click on Hazardous Waste, under Quick Links.

Right-to-Know Hazardous Substances Fact Sheets

The New Jersey Department of Health and Human Services has recently published a collection of "fact sheets" on substances—both inside and outside the home—harmful to human health and the environment.

These detailed fact sheets cover acute health effects, chronic health effects, and tips on limiting exposure. If you want facts about specific chemicals, New Jersey has answers for you at www.state.nj.us/health/eoh/rtkweb/newenglish.htm.

The World Health Organization

The World Health Organization, www.who.org, is your source for information on a huge variety of topics relating to public health, including worldwide rates of cancer, AIDS, and other epidemics. Along with SEER (http://seer.cancer.gov/), the WHO produces the definitive report on cancer statistics both in this country and abroad.

The Centers for Disease Control and Prevention

The Centers for Disease Control and Prevention, a branch of the U.S. Department of Health and Human Services that frequently works with the WHO, has several valuable resources. You can find information on public health and the role of toxins in our lives through these branches of the CDC: The National Center for Health Statistics, "National Health Information Survey," www.cdc.gov/nchs and the Agency for Toxic Substances and Disease Registry, www.atsdr.cdc.gov.

The National Resources Defense Council

The National Resources Defense Council (www.nrdc.org) is a nationwide environmental action organization—probably the most respected in the country. Its Web site is a reliable source of information on everything from global warming to environmental law.

National Safety Council

Some of my general definitions came from the National Safety Council's glossary (www.nsc.org/ehc/glossar2.htm). You can find a lot of great facts on environmental topics here.

Children's Environmental Health/Studies on Children's Health

My Web site, www.dienviro.com, has a lot of great information for people interested in learning more about the state of our children's health. In particular I recommend these links:

Children's Environmental Health
    Coalition
www.chccblog.org

EPA Children's Health Protection
www.yosemite.epa.gov/ochp/
    ochpweb.nsf/content/homepage
    .htm

National Institute of Health:
    Children's Environmental
    Health Conference
www.nih.gov/

American Academy of Pediatrics
www.aap.org/

Asthma and Allergy Foundation of
    America
www.aafa.org/

Holistic Moms Network
www.holisticmoms.org/

Tomorrow's Children's Fund
www.atcfkid.com/

Tomorrow's Children's Institute
www.tcikids.com/

National Childhood Cancer
    Foundation
www.curesearch.org

Works Cited

In addition to the resources listed above and ones mentioned in the text, I have referred to the following texts:

Chlorine Bleach
T. L. Litovitz, "2000 AAPCC Annual Report," *American Journal of Emergency Medicine*, Vol. 19, No. 5, September 2001.
Agency for Toxic Substances and Disease Registry, "Medical Management Guidelines for Chlorine," Division of Toxicology, U.S. Department of Health and Human Services, 2003.
R. D. Morris et al., "Chlorination, Chlorination By-Products, and Cancer: A Meta-Analysis," *American Journal of Public Health*, Vol. 87, No. 7, 1992, pp. 955–63.

Asthma

The National Heart, Lung, and Blood Institute, *Guidelines for the Diagnosis and Management of Asthma*, National Institutes of Health Publication No. 97-4051, 1991.

The American Thoracic Society, "Future Directions for Research on Diseases of the Lung," *American Journal of Respiratory and Critical Care Medicine*, February 1998.

Childhood Cancer

The Natural Resources Defense Council, "Children, Cancer, and the Environment," www.nrdc.org/health/kids/kidscancer/kidscancer1.asp

The Centers for Disease Control and Prevention, "Vital and Health Statistics, National Hospital Discharge Survey: Annual Summary 1993," DHHS Publication No. PHS 95-1782, 1995.

Marilyn Massey-Stokes and Beth Lanning, "Childhood Cancer and Environmental Toxins: The Debate Continues," *Family and Community Health*, January 2002.

National Cancer Institute, *Understanding Gene Testing*, National Institutes of Health Publication No. 96-3905, 1995.

M. J. Friedrich, "Lowering Risk of the Second Malignancy in the Survivors of Childhood Cancer," *Journal of American Medical Association*, May 2001.

Tami Gouveia-Viegant et al., "Toxic Chemicals and Childhood Cancer: A Review of the Evidence," University of Massachusetts at Lowell, May 2003.

Birth Defects

Jane Houlihan et al., "Body Burden: The Pollution in Newborns," *Environmental Working Group*, July 2005.

Beate Ritz et al., "Ambient Air Pollution and Risk of Birth Defects in Southern California," *Journal of American Epidemiology*, vol. 155, No. 1, 2002.

Developmental Disorders
Michael Szpir, "Tracing the Origins of Autism," *Environmental Health Perspectives*, July 2006.

Indoor Air Pollution
EPA Indoor Environments Division, "Indoor Air Quality Tools for Schools: Actions to Improve IAQ," September 1999.
EPA Indoor Environments Division, "Indoor Air Quality and Student Performance," August 2000.

The Science of Housekeeping
Cleaning 101, the Soap and Detergent Association, http://cleaning101.com.

Tier System
U.S. Department of the Interior, "Guidance and Training on Greening Your Janitorial Business," www.doi.gov/greening/sustain/final2.html.

Petroleum Distillates
Marilyn Smith, "The Mechanism of Benzene-induced Leukemia: A Hypothesis and Speculations on the Causes of Leukemia," *Environmental Health Perspectives*, February 1997.

Artificial Fragrances
"Neurotoxins: At Home and the Workplace," Report by the Committee on Science and Technology, U.S. House of Representatives, Sept. 16, 1986, Report 99-827.

Houseplants

NASA and the Associated Landscape Contractors of America, Environmental Assurance Program, http://www.ssc.nasa.gov/environmental/docforms/water_research/water_research.html.

Dioxin and Triclosan

"Dioxin: EPA's Reassessment of Dioxin Health Effects and Estimates of Exposure," www.epa.gov/ord/researchaccomplishments/dioxin.html.

Christian Daughton et al., "Pharmaceuticals and Personal Care Products in the Environment: Agents of Subtle Change?" *Environmental Health Perspectives*, December 1999.

Karen Gilbert, "Potential Consequences of Antibacterial Product Use Need Reassessment," *Virginia Tech News*, April 2006.

Steve Karnowski, "Sunlight Converts Common Antibacterial to Dioxin," *Associated Press*, 14 April 2003.